Reel Big Bullies

Transgressions: Cultural Studies and Education

Series Editor

Shirley R. Steinberg (*University of Calgary, Canada*)

Founding Editor

Joe L. Kincheloe (1950–2008) (*The Paulo and Nita Freire International Project for Critical Pedagogy*)

Editorial Board

Rochelle Brock (*University of North Carolina, Greensboro, USA*)
Annette Coburn (*University of the West of Scotland, UK*)
Kenneth Fasching-Varner (*Louisiana State University, USA*)
Luis Huerta-Charles (*New Mexico State University, USA*)
Christine Quail (*McMaster University, Canada*)
Jackie Seidel (*University of Calgary, Canada*)
Cathryn Teasley (*University of A Coruña, Spain*)
Sandra Vega (*IPEC Instituto de Pedagogía Crítica, Mexico*)
Mark Vicars (*Victoria University, Queensland, Australia*)

This book series is dedicated to the radical love and actions of Paulo Freire, Jesus "Pato" Gomez, and Joe L. Kincheloe.

VOLUME 129

The titles published in this series are listed at *brill.com/tcse*

Reel Big Bullies

Teaching to the Problem

By

Brian C. Johnson
James E. Vines

BRILL
SENSE

LEIDEN | BOSTON

All chapters in this book have undergone peer review.

The Library of Congress Cataloging-in-Publication Data is available online at http://catalog.loc.gov

Typeface for the Latin, Greek, and Cyrillic scripts: "Brill". See and download: brill.com/brill-typeface.

ISSN 2214-9732
ISBN 978-90-04-38489-7 (paperback)
ISBN 978-90-04-38493-4 (hardback)
ISBN 978-90-04-38494-1 (e-book)

Copyright 2018 by Koninklijke Brill NV, Leiden, The Netherlands.
Koninklijke Brill NV incorporates the imprints Brill, Brill Hes & De Graaf, Brill Nijhoff, Brill Rodopi, Brill Sense, Hotei Publishing, mentis Verlag, Verlag Ferdinand Schöningh and Wilhelm Fink Verlag.
All rights reserved. No part of this publication may be reproduced, translated, stored in a retrieval system, or transmitted in any form or by any means, electronic, mechanical, photocopying, recording or otherwise, without prior written permission from the publisher.
Authorization to photocopy items for internal or personal use is granted by Koninklijke Brill NV provided that the appropriate fees are paid directly to The Copyright Clearance Center, 222 Rosewood Drive, Suite 910, Danvers, MA 01923, USA. Fees are subject to change.

This book is printed on acid-free paper and produced in a sustainable manner.

Contents

Foreword VII
Cathy S. Keegan
Preface IX

1 **Bully**
 Introduction 1

2 **Read It and Weep**
 Stats about Bullying 13

3 **Dazed & Confused**
 Defining Bullying 16

4 **The Little Rascals**
 Memorable Movie Bullies 19

5 **See No Evil, Hear No Evil**
 Changing Bystander Attitudes 29

6 **Dangerous Minds**
 Prevailing Attitudes about Bullying Culture 32

7 **It's a Mad, Mad, Mad World**
 Mean World Syndrome (Media Effects) 36

8 **Advise & Consent**
 Legal Policy and Bullying 43

9 **Lean on Me**
 The Role of the Teacher as Intervener 51

10 **The Big Short**
 Film Clips for Instructional Use 60

11 **This Is the End**
    Conclusion   142

   Film Index   145
   Films by Definition   147
   Term Index   150

Foreword

As a superintendent in public education, I believe educators and administrators need to take an active role responding to accepted cultural behaviors such as bullying. More than ever, children are entering and existing inside and outside of our American schools under duress. I define duress as those students who are victims of social, emotional, physical, verbal, and cyber bullying, including intimidation, hazing, humiliation, harassment, discrimination, social exclusion, bias, revenge and bystander effect. As a school leader, I view these accepted behaviors as unacceptable, acknowledging it is imperative that they are addressed at school. Our children can learn a new way to interact with each other. The school can serve as place that embraces a culture of affirmation, not fear and destruction. As educators, we have a job to do. Our job is to eliminate bullying entirely by creating a generation of individuals who do not accept this antisocial behavior. State legislators and Departments of Education recognize the implications of bullying and mandate bullying policies. Teachers need the resources, research, curricula and pedagogy to effectively respond as "front line" interventionists to reshape student behaviors, beliefs and attitudes.

In order to affect this change, trusting relationships need to be formed between teachers and students. Additionally, school systems must adopt resources such as character and citizenship curricula, bullying programs, and use teaching tools such as movies to strengthen the understanding of the inferences of bullying, and identify replacement behaviors. To all, movies are a familiar medium that create comfort and relatability, yet they have the power to reshape one's thinking.

This most recent work of Dr. Brian Johnson and his colleague, Dr. James Vines, could play a significant role in helping our schools and teachers to understand the power of film to address bullying. The authors note that film increases student engagement, complements instruction, and promotes interaction and higher order thinking skills. Specifically, as a member of our school community and well respected faith based leader, it is known that Dr. Johnson and Dr. Vines understand bullying and bullying archetypes. He recognizes that on a daily basis our children face being bullied because of race, sexual orientation, gender identity, and religious preferences. As experts and well-known figures in our community, Dr. Johnson and Dr. Vines passionately advocate for the elimination of bullying. In this book, *Reel Big Bullies: Teaching to the Problem* both authors present the reader with resources, research, curriculum guides and teaching strategies, all aligned to bullying behaviors within popular movies. I highly recommend this read to all educators. We have a social responsibility to address undesirable bullying behaviors exhibited by our students, within our schools and classrooms. This book can help us meet that goal.

Cathy S. Keegan
Superintendent of Milton (PA) Area School District
January 2018

Preface

Bullying was once considered a normal, inevitable part of growing up. Boys hitting each other on the playground were shrugged off with the thought that "boys will be boys." Girls excluding one another were considered to be engaging in a rite of passage to womanhood. National incidents like school shootings at Columbine High or at Virginia Tech and the rash of suicides of gay teens and college students have cast new light on the age-old problem of bullying. In these cases, the perpetrators were themselves victims of bullying or had felt the stinging effects of social isolation and discrimination.

Bullying at school means that learning occurs in a culture of fear and intimidation. Defining bullying is a first step towards understanding it. Bullying occurs "when one or more persons repeatedly say or do hurtful things to another person who has problems defending himself or herself," according to the US Department of Health and Human Services. These attacks can include taunting, teasing, hitting, threatening, or indirect bullying through purposeful exclusion caused by gossip and rumors.

Rightfully so, educators must confront the bullying culture rampant in American schools. Not only must they address the negative behaviors, but they must also empower those who are being victimized and those who feel powerless to affect change.

Bullying behavior is frequently a subject in popular culture artifacts, particularly movies. A recent search of the keyword on the Internet Movie Database (www.imdb.com) and on Netflix revealed over two thousand movie titles of all genres—even for children. Given Hollywood's penchant for the subject, is it any wonder that our children believe such behavior is normal and to be expected? Cultivation theory suggests that such significant and prolonged exposure to these themes may be having a profound and detrimental effect on kids' expectations of the way life *should* be.

In a recent course on bullying at a public university taught by one of the authors of this book, three themes continuously emerged among the student population: (a) there's nothing anyone can do about it, (b) bullying is necessary as it builds character, and (c) there needs to be more educational programming in the schools designed to curb bullying behavior.

Contest
(Contest LLC, 2013)
2:28–4:01

Contrast these sentiments with the helplessness teachers and administrators feel. Many will tell you that current state and federal guidelines tie their hands until after an incident occurs. In other words, a student must get hurt before the school is able to do anything. *Reel Big Bullies: Teaching to the*

Problem is designed for regular anti-bullying campaigns and will not cost struggling districts thousands of dollars to implement as it provides teachers with educational resources to complement regular instruction in classrooms.

School districts across the country spend thousands of dollars annually to participate in campaigns designed to curb the problem with bullying in schools. They bring in high-paid consultants who make great promises about how their canned programs will work to change student behaviors. Superintendents who recognize the problem are anxious and hopeful to find the solution—just one thing—that will keep another child from being hurt, from being ostracized, and hopefully avoid something as terrible as a suicide or school shooting.

Regrettably, these administrators fail to recognize the greatest assets (tools/ "weapons" in the anti-bullying arsenal) they already possess in their districts— their teachers. Schools already have the best resources in the classrooms every day. These highly educated, credentialed, creative talents should be put to use every day—not just during a special week. Teachers are the best line of defense for students because they are already the eyes and ears of the school— capable of affecting the student culture daily—our goal is to give them the tools to do so.

Real Big Bullies: Teaching to the Problem is designed to help students, administrators, teachers and counselors create a safer school environment for all students. It is also intended to help all students understand the terrible toll bullying can take on its victims, and to encourage students to stand up for their classmates who are being harassed. The idea of putting others down, physically assaulting, or social excluding others has been normalized in the films we watch, and we have been desensitized to believe that bullying and hazing are a part of making the target a "better person." Developing an integrative approach using film will challenge participants to see the personhood and humanity of all persons, and to learn how to eliminate bystander behavior. *Reel Big Bullies: Teaching to the Problem* is designed to strengthen communities, foster mutual respect and build truly inclusive environments where all can thrive!

CHAPTER 1

Bully
Introduction

In addition to focusing on reading, writing, and math skills, educators have an opportunity to help students advance their critical thinking about alternative texts like movies. Mainstream Hollywood film is an excellent tool for teaching, but students must understand movies as harbingers of cultural expectations and beliefs, and not just entertainment. This introduction reviews pertinent literature relating film pedagogy and Bloom's taxonomy of educational objectives.

> **Bullying Survey**
>
> An exercise you can do with your students is the bullying survey. This introductory exercise can be used to assess your students' experiences with bullying.
> https://www.tolerance.org/classroom-resources/tolerance-lessons/a-bullying-survey

In the 2012 hit movie *Pitch Perfect,* Jesse (Skylar Astin) tries to woo Beca (Anna Kendrick), who loves music but who is unimpressed by Jesse's love of movies, particularly because of Hollywood's penchant for the predictable. He was incredulous and equated her position with "not liking puppies." He suggested she was in need of a "moviecation" to understand the ways that movies "bring people to tears" and how filmmakers "blow their minds." Jesse was on to something—movies are a part of our culture, and to understand how we come to understand ourselves, we must understand the power of film as a shaper of personal and societal identities.

In secondary and higher education, the push for students to learn critical, higher order thinking skills follows Bloom's taxonomy of educational objectives (Bloom, Engelhart, Furst, Hill, & Krathwohl, 1956). This taxonomy presents learning as a multi-tiered and hierarchical structure: [from lowest to highest] knowledge, comprehension, application, analysis, synthesis, and evaluation. Each of these is situated in the affective, cognitive, and psychomotor domains. The taxonomy presents a systematic process of alignment between standards and educational goals, objectives, products, and activities.

Widely recognized as a classification system for establishing learning outcomes for students, Bloom's taxonomy provides a core lexicon for educators. The taxonomy primarily covers two domains: cognitive and affective. The cognitive domain primarily refers to mental information processing that does not relate to emotions or feelings; the affective domain speaks to those emotional and subjective values and feelings. Regardless of domain area, the educational objectives range from lower order to higher order—from simple to complex, from recall to critical thinking and problem solving. Higher order activities are, ideally, the preferred trajectory for learning in higher education as to reach these levels, students must be actively engaged and committed to learning (Lewis & Smith, 1993). These activities tend to be transformative and experiential.

Bloom et al. (1956) created this taxonomy as a classification system that made learning objectives clear and meaningful; provided for reliable testing and evaluation measures; and facilitated the development of new learning theories (Chyung, 2008). Bloom and his colleagues initially outlined their hierarchical cognitive goals (focused primarily on developing intellectual skills) from knowledge to synthesis and evaluation.

Similarly, the framework for learning in the affective domain proffers a hierarchical structure regarding what can be described as intangibles (emotions, values, and attitudes). These included concepts like awareness, and affirmation.

The taxonomy was designed to emphasize the importance of complexity of learning and effectiveness of teaching. The addition of instructional media opened opportunities to add to that complexity. For numerous years, the use of audiovisual aids like photographs, dioramas, slide projectors, and filmstrips were the primary method of introducing media for instructional purposes (Garrison & Akyol, 2009). The following section describes the educational benefits and outcomes of using film as an instructional tool in manners consistent with Bloom's cognitive and affective domains.

Bloom & Film Pedagogy

The primary objective of this section is to examine the literature on the usefulness of using the medium of mainstream Hollywood film as a part of instructional pedagogy, particularly applying the literature to the domains of Bloom's (1956) taxonomy of student learning. Film has been found effective in both the cognitive and affective domains. As a popular medium, film has the potential to have both entertainment and educational value; and according to recent research, both are necessary and beneficial in the classroom.

For decades, classroom instruction has employed a traditional lecture format where the teacher imparts information and students become receptacles (Berrett, 2012). In recent years, traditionalism has been challenged as educational research has stressed the need for students to be more involved in the creation of knowledge and to be recognized for already having ways of knowing that are important to the course content. Film pedagogy has been advanced as a promising method of facilitating classroom communication by offering instructors a more interactive, student centered classroom experience (Briley, 2002). Movies are already a popular medium, and their pervasiveness has the potential to create a classroom consensus that is so important for deeper and sustained dialogue. Film offers benefits for all learning domains: cognitive, affective, and behavioral; as students grow in their knowledge, motivation, and skills, the potential for enhancing group communication in classrooms grows exponentially.

Using Film for Cognitive Development

The cognitive domain (Bloom et al., 1956) involves knowledge and the development of intellectual skills. This includes the recall or recognition of specific facts, procedural patterns, and concepts that serve in the development of intellectual abilities and skills.

Using film to enhance classroom instruction benefits students' cognition by increasing memory (English & Nielson, 2010), providing visual cues (Hansen, 1933), promoting student engagement and connection to the course content (Butler, Zaromb, Lyle, & Roediger, 2009), which increases retention of materials and fosters critical thinking (Lip & Li, 2010).

Integrating movie clips into instruction promotes memory and recall of information. Film in the classroom improves retention of information by providing strong images and emotional content; these viewed cues then become pathways for students to internalize the information and to be able to remember important details. English and Nielson (2010) showed that those students who exhibited higher arousal retained information better and were able to reject misinformation at higher levels than those in the control group.

Hansen (1933) argued that "without exception" (p. 1) moving pictures are proven tools to promote learning. Findings showed that students retained the information longer when it was related to video content. As students are able to retain more information, their attention and engagement increases. Through use of film clips, learners develop increased linkages between story details and related course content; in turn, fostering creativity by stimulating the flow of ideas for classroom discussion or in written activities (Butler et al., 2009).

Butler et al. (2009) studied learning from fictional films; participants read shorter texts about topics from historical record and then watched clips from related fictional films. Participants were able to more often produce the correct answers to questions when they read the text and were shown correct information from the film over when they read the text alone. Results show that viewing films containing correct and incorrect information has both positive and negative impact on student learning.

Lip and Li (2010) found that attending to film pedagogy allows for the transfer of critical thinking skills to assorted situations. The researchers required students to complete reflective questionnaires aimed at understanding if the films were interesting and engaging. In follow-up interviews students identified that the films were useful for critical analysis skills.

Barnett and Kafka (2007) argue that because students (aged 10–22) spend at minimum three hours weekly watching movies and eight hours watching television, college science courses should teach students to critically evaluate the science-related media. They argue that one advantage of film pedagogy helps students "avoid the disconnect that often occurs when students learn a concept and then are expected to apply that concept in real-world situations" (p. 32). Results indicated that the use of film clips were effective in promoting both student interest in and understanding of course content.

In the end, film in the classroom not only increases students' retention of information, but students are more likely then to understand the course content, which increases the likelihood that learning in the affective domain is also being enhanced.

The Affective Domain and Film

The affective domain includes factors such as student motivation, attitudes, perceptions and values (Hart, 1989). Teachers can increase their effectiveness by considering the affective domain in planning courses, delivering lectures and activities, and assessing student learning. Incorporating film clips into classroom instruction has the potential to significantly impact students' disposition towards classroom attendance, interest, and can serve as a catalyst to increased involvement by students.

Developing a classroom community is one approach that enhances affective learning. One of the immediate benefits of instructional pedagogies with film is that movie watching is mostly a communal experience. Jowett and Linton (1980) argue that movies create a type of "visual public consensus" (p. 75). They speak to the power of film to bypass traditional forces of socialization and education (family, church, school) and establish immediate relational contact with the watcher. Film engages a wide audience, cuts to the heart of issues quickly and provides an accessible meeting place for people of different backgrounds. Because of this, movies serve as a vehicle for collaboration, helping to build the connections with other students and the instructor.

The idea of developing a community of learners has been shown to positively effect upon social factors, cognition, and teaching efficacy. McKinney, McKinney, Franiuk, and Schweitzer (2006) measured students' satisfaction throughout a semester long psychology course in relation to students' experience of classroom community. Summers and Svinicki (2007) examined the links between classroom community and student motivation; their study showed how interactive classrooms and collaborative learning affected student motivation and performance in higher degrees than for students in traditional lecture-style classes. These findings confirm Rovai's (2002) study that when learners "feel a sense of community, it is possible that this emotional connectedness may provide the support needed for them not only to complete successfully a class or a program, but also to learn more" (p. 321).

It is important to grab a student's attention as a part of the learning process (Keller, 1987). By using feature films in class, faculty members grab students' attention, inspire, and motivate students. Berk (2009) suggests a framework for incorporating film clips and other multimedia into the classroom to draw on various learning styles and multiple intelligences. Auerbach (2012) suggests an interactive approach to classroom content; film can energize a learning situation. Smith, Cavanaugh, and Moore (2011) found that students in the multimedia groups reported studying more and suggesting that videos facilitated information processing thereby enhancing student self-efficacy. That sense of anticipation fosters more positive attitudes about course content.

As faculty members are able to increase student engagement and motivation, students' attitudes towards content and learning become much more positive. Using film becomes a catalyst to decreasing students' anxiety and tension about tougher subjects like diversity (Barkley, 2009). To promote learning, educators should identify components of instruction that increase learning motivation, allowing students to be provoked to pursue and use knowledge and skills (Butler et al., 2009).

Psychomotor Skills as Disciplinary Application

The psychomotor domain traditionally entails behavioral skills development. Similarly, hierarchical, psychomotor skills involve: imitation, manipulation, precision, articulation, and naturalization—often centered on physical activity. Involvement in sports, doing scientific experiments, making group or individual presentations, and role-play are often considered in the affective domain (Rupani & Bhutto, 2011). As the concept of psychomotor skills relates to skills development, this section will review how film is used instructionally to help students build specific skills within varied disciplines.

Film has grown in popularity for classroom use, and while not all university educators have embraced movie pedagogy, some faculty members argue that it has revolutionized classroom teaching within discipline.

One such manner that film integrates with discipline specific teaching is in providing outside of textbook learning for fields where human interaction is necessary. Theology educators use film as a way of broadening students' understanding of the connection of theological studies to other areas of life, and in doing so, making those who practice ministry more grounded with people (Snyder, 2007; Mercadante, 2007). In allied health careers, moving pictures allow for a humanistic approach to experiential learning where characters can represent real-life patients for situational learning (Herrman, 2006). Additionally, medical students can learn professionalism as they study film representations; Lumlertgul, Kijpaisalratana, Pityaratstian, and Wangsaturaka (2009) used film to teach students in medical education courses about the ethics of care, gaining informed consent, and moral and critical thinking.

These same benefits have been found by social work educators who use film scenes as case studies (Liles, 2007). In his theoretical essay, Liles (2007) highlights the effective use of film in social work education as it prepares students for real-world application. He contends that film can be used as methods to evaluate specific characters and how to potentially work with them to consider how social work is represented as a profession. He also highlights how film can be used as a therapeutic tool itself in work with real clients.

In addition to the human touch, some fields use film as a way of extending theory into practice. The business fields use film, but they also integrate television clips, animations, and other increasingly popular media to illustrate the full spectrum of business-related topics (Smith, 2009). Some use film as the primary instructional strategy, effectively eliminating student textbooks (Leet & Houser, 2003). In economics, educators have used film to exemplify how economics is "relevant to virtually every aspect of their everyday lives" (Sexton, 2006, p. 417). Parker (2009) extends this idea of the usefulness of film in illustrating concepts in management. The idea of film connecting to the everyday lived experience of students has been shown valuable in multiple fields, despite being merely fictional sources.

Fictional Sources & Attitude Change

The use of fictional sources (film, literature, television, etc.) in the classroom has been shown to be valuable as a method to support learning of course content.

Studies suggest the factors affecting learning from fictional sources includes the learner's age (younger students tend to learn from fictional sources), prior knowledge (what learners bring to the text does not "protect" (Nielsen, 2010, p. 458) them from misinformation present in fictional source), and need for cognition (determined by individuals who preference higher order, more complex problems—these students tend to are more likely to distrust fictional sources). Consistent with the literature on learning, short-term interventions (single, brief exposure) showed the long and short-term effects on learning. Because films are "rich in visual and auditory information" (p. 463), students tend to be able to recall information more than traditional texts.

Gerrig and Prentice (1991) sought to understand whether information from fictional narratives like those in movies and books are integrated into consumers' real-life knowledge base. Results showed that fictional information sometimes "creates inappropriate states of the world" (p. 338) that do not necessarily become embedded into long-term memory in the same way as factual information.

Busselle and Bilandzic (2008) provides a theoretical framework that attempts to explain the effect of perceptions of "unrealness" in the critical engagement of learners dealing with fictional sources, particularly upon transportation and identification with central characters. They explain a process by which transportation in interpreted by a loss of self and the real world. According to their mental model, transportation and engagement with narrative happens regardless of medium (print, television, film). Like Marsh, Butler, and Umanath (2012), these authors postulate that in order to be transported, individuals must be willing to suspend disbelief in the fictionality of a text. Their contention is that "texts are approached with initial credulity and not with incredulity, unless otherwise prompted" (p. 265). Viewers of film texts or readers of printed texts must distinguish between external realism judgments (defined as the decision where what is fictional approaches real world) or relative realism where audiences accept even unlikely narrative circumstances that are not within their sense of reality by judging the relative plausibility as consistent with what *could be*. Regarding transportation, Busselle and Bilandzic (2008) recognize that viewers' predispositions and preferences towards genre, authors, actors, or moods may interrupt audience engagement with the text.

Green, Garst, and Brock (2004) support the notion that fictional literature and film sources can influence viewers' attitudes. The authors provide a theoretical framework that attempts to explain two potential mechanisms that undergird fictional communication: low elaborative scrutiny and high experienced transportation. Low elaborative scrutiny suggests that consumers of fictional materials are less likely to critically think about or scrutinize fictional content than non-fictional. Similarly, individuals who are highly transported into a fiction narrative are those who read the content as having high personal relevance. Their review suggests that individuals are willing to "alter their real-world beliefs" (p. 173) in response to fictional narratives, particularly those that engage the reader/viewer through cognitive, emotional, and mental pathways.

In their essay examining the psychological processes affecting a narrative's impact, Gerring and Rapp (2004) question the extent to which an individual reader's transportation into a narrative world is able to change the person's attitudes and beliefs. Consistent with other literature on transportation, they suggest that those who report greater experiences of transportation experience deeper impact on their attitudes or beliefs. Students saw "belief change" (p. 269) more significantly for stories that were not based at their own institutions. To measure transportation effect, the researchers used the transportation scale measure of Green and Brock (2000) to examine whether respondents could picture the events of the narrative actually happening or could see themselves within the narrative situation.

Conclusion

Wheeler and Davoust (1994) argues against the using of video in the classroom purely for entertainment purposes. They suggest that when media is used in classes as a complement or reinforcement for class lessons, it is more effective. They preference curriculum-based videos over entertainment media, but describe a process by which teachers should choose which media is most appropriate. They suggest the importance of: having a comprehensive plan for how the media is connected to the curriculum; media that promotes problem-solving inquiry; and, a strong connection between the audio and video that holds students' interests.

Similarly, Stoddard and Marcus (2010) outline strategies to encourage teachers to incorporate film in the history classroom as a method of increasing student engagement and understanding of content. The authors identify a list of films that are useful in teaching historical subjects related to racial issues and stereotyping, issues related to wars and militarism, and other historical issues. They proffer that teachers must have a clear purpose for using a particular film and that they make sure that the film is consistent with course goals or learning objectives.

Marcus, Paxton, and Meyerson (2006) believe that students learn much from popular media—even how to "make meaning of their lives" (p. 517), but suggest that not enough literature exists to explain what they learn. They question how students' "ideas about history are indeed shaped 'at the movies'" (p. 519).

This review includes an examination of research on using film media in classroom instruction through the lens of the historical frameworks of instructional technology paying particular attention to how film pedagogy fits within Bloom's taxonomy of educational objectives. Bloom is widely accepted in higher education as the model for learning goals and outcomes. The review includes a discussion of the cognitive, behavioral, and affective domains and the benefits for faculty who have adopted film pedagogy to complement instruction. Relatedly, this chapter reviews research and invites faculty to consider how viewing films influences a person's sense of self and how it affects a person's values and beliefs despite being fictional sources.

Another feature of *Reel Big Bullies: Teaching to the Problem* is an extensive section on designing an anti-bullying education campaign using mainstream Hollywood film as the vehicle—right in your classroom. Teachers will benefit from the classroom teaching ideas including suggested instructional activities, recommended readings, possible assignments, and advice on creating a classroom atmosphere for tough, sometimes politically and emotionally charged topics. These suggestions are accompanied by highlighted lesson plans found online (link included) that outline student learning opportunities.

Rather than just being another book on film literacy, theory, and criticism, this resource manual stands out from the competitors for its practical, user friendly mini-lessons using film clips from mainstream Hollywood feature films from a variety of genres. The lessons in this book are designed to supplement instruction on bullying issues. For each term in the list of definitions, we have provided a movie clip that illustrates the concept being taught. Each clip lasts no longer than ten minutes in length. With nearly 200 clips of all genres for age levels elementary through high school, both novice and experienced educators will find visual illustrations to supplement their instruction.

In this text, there is intentional integration of film clips into the book's narrative; these recommended clips provide a user-friendly option to highlight important topics. Another feature includes call-outs that highlight various resources: video documentaries, books in print, websites, or films that provide additional support for the subject being discussed. These resources offer opportunities to go deeper into a lesson or to provide an activity for student learning.

References

Auerbach, A. H. (2012). Teaching diversity: Using a multifaceted approach to engage students. *PS: Political Science & Politics, 45*(3), 516–520.

Barkley, E. F. (2009). *Student engagement techniques: A handbook for college faculty.* San Francisco, CA: Jossey-Bass.

Barnett, M., & Kafka, A. (2007). Using science fiction movie scenes to support critical analysis of science. *Journal of College Science Teaching, 36*(4), 31.

Berk, R. A. (2009). Multimedia teaching with video clips: TV, movies, YouTube, and mtvU in the college classroom. *International Journal of Technology in Teaching and Learning, 5*(1), 1–21.

Berrett, D. (2012). How 'flipping' the classroom can improve the traditional lecture. *The Chronicle of Higher Education, 12,* 1–14.

Bloom, B. S., Engelhart, M. D., Furst, F. J., Hill, W. H., & Krathwohl, D. R. (1956). *Taxonomy of educational objectives: The classification of education goals.* New York, NY: Longman.

Boud, D., Cohen, R., & Sampson, J. (Eds.). (2014). *Peer learning in higher education: Learning from and with each other.* London: Routledge.

Briley, R. (2002). Teaching film and history. *OAH Magazine of History, 16*(4), 3–4.

Busselle, R., & Bilandzic, H. (2008). Fictionality and perceived realism in experiencing stories: A model of narrative comprehension and engagement. *Communication Theory, 18*(2), 255–280.

Butler, A. C., Zaromb, F. M., Lyle, K. B., & Roediger, H. L. (2009). Using popular films to enhance classroom learning the good, the bad, and the interesting. *Psychological Science, 20*(9), 1161–1168.

Chyung, S. Y. (2008). *Foundations of instructional performance technology.* Amherst, MA: HRD Press.

English, S. M., & Nielson, K. A. (2010). Reduction of the misinformation effect by arousal induced after learning. *Cognition, 117*(2), 237–242.

Garrison, D. R., & Akyol, Z. (2009). Role of instructional technology in the transformation of higher education. *Journal of Computing in Higher Education, 21*(1), 19–30.

Gerrig, R. J., & Prentice, D. A. (1991). The representation of fictional information. *Psychological Science, 2*(5), 336–340.

Gerring, R. J., & Rapp, D. (2004). Psychological processes underlying literary impact. *Poetics Today, 25*(2), 265–281.

Green, M. C., & Brock, T. C. (2000). The role of transportation in the persuasiveness of public narratives. *Journal of Personality and Social Psychology, 79*(5), 701.

Green, M. C., Garst, J., & Brock, T. C. (2004). The power of fiction: Determinants and boundaries. In L. J. Shrum (Ed.), *The psychology of entertainment media: Blurring the lines between entertainment and persuasion* (pp. 161–176). Mahwah, NJ: Lawrence Erlbaum Associates.

Hansen, J. E. (1933). The effect of educational motion pictures upon the retention of informational learning. *The Journal of Experimental Education, 2*(1), 1–4.

Hart, L. E. (1989). Describing the affective domain: Saying what we mean. In D. B. Mcleod & V. M. Adams (Eds.), *Affect and mathematical problem solving* (pp. 37–45). New York, NY: Springer-Verlag.

Hart, R. (2010). Classroom behaviour management: Educational psychologists' views on effective practice. *Emotional and Behavioural Difficulties, 15*(4), 353–371.

Herrman, J. W. (2006). Using film clips to enhance nursing education. *Nurse Educator, 31*(6), 264–269.

Jowett, G., & Linton, J. M. (1980). *Movies as mass communication*. Beverly Hills, CA: Sage Publications.

Keller, J. M. (1987). Development and use of the ARCS model of instructional design. *Journal of Instructional Development, 10*(3), 2–10.

Leet, D., & Houser, S. (2003). Economics goes to hollywood: Using classic films and documentaries to create an undergraduate economics course. *The Journal of Economic Education, 34*(4), 326–332.

Lewis, A., & Smith, D. (1993). Defining higher order thinking. *Theory into Practice, 32*(3), 131–137.

Liles, R. E. (2007). The use of feature films as teaching tools in social work education. *Journal of Teaching in Social Work, 27*(3–4), 45–60.

Lumlertgul, N., Kijpaisalratana, N., Pityaratstian, N., & Wangsaturaka, D. (2009). Cinemeducation: A pilot student project using movies to help students learn medical professionalism. *Medical Teacher, 31*(7), e327–e332.

Marcus, A. S., Paxton, R. J., & Meyerson, P. (2006). "The reality of it all": History students read the movies. *Theory & Research in Social Education, 34*(4), 516–552.

Marsh, E. J., Butler, A. C., & Umanath, S. (2012). Using fictional sources in the classroom: Applications from cognitive psychology. *Educational Psychology Review, 24*(3), 449–469.

McKinney, J. P., McKinney, K. G., Franiuk, R., & Schweitzer, J. (2006). The college classroom as a community: Impact on student attitudes and learning. *College Teaching, 54*(3), 281–284.

Mercadante, L. (2007). Using film to teach theology. *Theological Education, 42*(2), 19–28.

Parker, R. D. (2009). Watch this clip: Using film as an augmentation to lecture and class discussion. *Academy of Educational Leadership Journal, 13*(4), 129.

Rovai, A. P. (2002). Building sense of community at a distance. *The International Review of Research in Open and Distributed Learning, 3*(1), 1–16. Retrieved from http://www.irrodl.org/index.php/irrodl/article/view/79/152

Rupani, C. M., & Bhutto, M. I. (2011). Evaluation of existing teaching learning process on bloom's taxonomy. *International Journal of Academic Research in Business and Social Sciences, 1*(3 Special), 109–118. Retrieved from http://www.hrmars.com/journals

Sexton, R. L. (2006). Using short movie and television clips in the economics principles class. *The Journal of Economic Education, 37*(4), 406–417.

Smith, A. R., Cavanaugh, C., & Moore, W. A. (2011). Instructional multimedia: An investigation of student and instructor attitudes and student study behavior. *BMC Medical Education, 11*(1), 1.

Smith, G. W. (2009). Using feature films as the primary instructional medium to teach organizational behavior. *Journal of Management Education, 33*(4), 462–489.

Snyder, S. (2007). The dangers of 'doing our duty' reflections on churches engaging with people seeking asylum in the UK. *Theology, 110*(857), 351–360.

Stoddard, J. D., & Marcus, A. S. (2010). More than "showing what happened": Exploring the potential of teaching history with film. *The High School Journal, 93*(2), 83–90.

Summers, J. J., & Svinicki, M. D. (2007). Investigating classroom community in higher education. *Learning and Individual Differences, 17*(1), 55–67.

Wheeler, R., & Davoust, D. (1994). Using film & video in the curriculum. *Media and Methods, 30*, 8.

CHAPTER 2

Read It and Weep
Stats about Bullying

The National Center for Education Statistics (NCES) provided data on students who were bullied at school. The students ranged from 12–18 to years old. The results showed that over 20% of students reported being a target of bullying at school (NCES, 2017). The center provided rates on the different way students experienced bullying. A small number of students, 1.8% reported having their property destroyed. A slightly larger number of students, 3.9% experienced threats of harm. Thirteen percent of students reported having rumors spread about them. The highest number came from students who reported being made fun of, called names or insulted (NCES, 2017). It is important to mention that the report included experiences, which occurred inside the school, on school property, the school bus as well as traveling to and from school.

> **Have a Heart Exercise**
>
> Students participate in an exercise where they learn about words and heartbreak.
> http://www.pbs.org/newshour/extra/app/uploads/2013/11/Bullying-Heart-Exercise-for-Individuals-final.pdf

The data from NCES illustrates that bullying continues to be an issue. Targets often experience social and verbal bullying. The impact of bullying is damaging and can leave both physical and emotional scars. Bullying targets often suffer from depression, low academic performance, avoiding school, low self-esteem, and have trouble building and maintaining friendships. Bullies often select targets based on physical appearance, or a difference in speech or behavior (Bullyingnoway.gov, 2017). Vulnerable populations such as minorities and students who are or perceived to be Lesbian, Gay, Bisexual and Transgendered (LGBT) report more bullying incidents that their peers (Bullyingnoway.gov, 2017).

> ***Three O'Clock High***
> (Amblin Entertainment, 1987)
> 14:09–18:31
>
> ***American Teen***
> (57th and Irving Productions, 2008)
> 25:54–29:04
>
> ***Unfriended***
> (Bazelevs Productions, 2014)
> 1:14:02–1:16:11

According to the National Center for Education Statistics 24.7% of African American students reported incidents of bullying, 17.2% for Hispanic students and 9% for Asian students. The number significantly increases for LGBT students. The data revealed that 74.1% of LGBT students were verbally bullied and 36.2% of LGBT students were physically bullied (National School Climate, 2013). The incidents of bullying lead to over half of self-identified or those perceived as LGBT students to feel unsafe attending schools. As mentioned earlier bullies tend to target those with differences particularly in physical or difference in speech. This makes students such as minorities who may look different due to their skin color, or have an accent. LGBT students may stand out if they do not adhere to traditional gender roles.

The information gathered from the National Center for Education Statistics reveals that many students can be at risk for being targets of bullying. One may wonder have these students always been at risk, or is this a recent phenomenon? Bullying has always been an issue in school but in recent years it has been pushed to the forefront. Our society has seen changes in how students interact, and communicate with each other. Before the age of technology, targets of bullies had the ability to escape once the school bell rang at 3:00. However, with the use of cellphone, computers, and videos uploads, targets of bullying can have their experiences shared and replayed by millions of people around the world.

Geography Club
(Enumerated Pictures, 2013)
48:37–50:03

Cursed
(Dimension Films, 2005)
2:39–4:29

Boys Don't Cry
(Fox Searchlight Pictures, 1999)
1:15:00–1:24:00

In recent years there has been a focus on bullying which occurs online. Students have the ability to take pictures, and record videos in school and upload them to social media. The students of today can log into their Twitter, Facebook, Youtube, and Snapchat channels and upload videos of the acts of bullying that occur inside the school walls. Prior to this technology parents, teachers and even student were not aware of an incident unless they were there to see it, or were told about the situation. Many students upload these videos in hopes of going viral, and possibly gaining Internet fame. We can all recall a time of hearing about a video posted online that gained media attention. Does anyone remember the Star Wars Kid? Fifteen year old Ghyslain Raza had a video released of him showing off his moves while pretending to be holding a lightsaber from *Star Wars*. The young man was bullied to the point he actually had to change schools. There have been countless videos of teens participating in fights, some which include multiple aggressors attacking one target. Recently, there was a video uploaded showing a group of Utah High School Cheerleaders chanting racial slurs (Huffingtonpost, 2017). These videos have a few things in common, for one they have an emotional impact on their targets. The videos make it difficult for the targets to feel comfortable going back to school or facing their peers as the video is being viewed by the world. These videos can also make for an unwelcoming school environment. While more and more videos are being uploaded, more data and research continues to be focused on the issues of cyberbullying.

Cyberbully
(Muse Entertainment, 2011)
40:27–43:02

Cyberbullying has been researched by Dr. Justin Patchin and Sameer Hinduja since 2002. Together they co-founded the Cyberbullying Research Center which is primarily focused on the causes, nature and consequences of cyberbullying. For the purpose of this book we are defining cyberbullying as the willful and repeated harm inflicted through the use of electronic devices (Hinduja & Patchin, 2014). The research from the Cyberbullying Research Center has shown that from 2007–2016 people who experienced cyberbullying has increased from 18 to 34 percent (Patchin & Hinduja, 2016).

References

Bullying No Way. (2017). *Diversity and bullying*. Retrieved from https://bullyingnoway.gov.au/UnderstandingBullying/WhyDoesBullyingHappen/Pages/Diversity-and-bullying.aspx

Hinduja, S., & Patchin, J. W. (2014). *Bullying beyond the schoolyeard: Preventing and responding to cyberbullying* (2nd ed.). Thousand Oaks, CA: Corwin Press.

National Center for Education Statistics (NCES). (2017). *Fast facts: Bullying*. Retrieved from https://nces.ed.gov/fastfacts/display.asp?id=719

Patchin, J. W., & Hinduja, S. (2016). *Summary of our cyberbullying research (2004–2016)*. Orlando, FL: Cyberbullying Research Center. Retrieved from http://cyberbullying.org/summary-of-our-cyberbullying-research

U.S. Department of Education, National Center for Education Statistics. (2017). *Indicators of school crime and safety*. Washington, DC: National Center for Education Statistics.

CHAPTER 3

Dazed & Confused
Defining Bullying

Bullying often comes in many forms. As mentioned in the previous chapter bullying can have lasting emotional and physical impact on both the bully and the target. Often times people may think they know what bullying looks like, but bullying morphs depending upon the context. The purpose of this chapter is to define specific terms relating to bullying that will help the reader throughout this book.

A Girl Like Her
(Radish Creative Group, 2015)
46:47–53:31

Glossary of Terms

Aggression Forceful action or unprovoked attack especially when intended to cause harm. Action is usually brought on by frustration.

Bias An inclination or preference either for or against an individual or group that interferes with an impartial judgment (prejudice).

Bullying Aggressive behavior occurring over a period of time with the intent to harm or disturb where there is an imbalance of power.

Cyberbullying The willful and repeated harm inflicted through the use of computers, cell phones, and other electronic devices.

Discrimination The denial of justice and fair treatment by both individuals and institutions in many arenas, including employment, education, housing, banking and political rights.

Harassment Harassment is unwelcome conduct that is based on race, color, religion, sex (including pregnancy), national origin, age (40 or older), disability or genetic information. Harassment becomes unlawful where (1) enduring the offensive conduct becomes a condition of continued employment, or (2) the conduct is severe or pervasive enough to create an environment that a reasonable person would consider intimidating, hostile, or abusive.

Hazing Any action taken or any situation created intentionally that causes embarrassment, harassment or ridicule and risks emotional and/or physical harm to members of a group or team, whether new or not, regardless of the person's willingness to participate.

Humiliation To cause someone to feel a loss of pride, dignity, or self-respect.

Offender The one who instigates social cruelty. Also known as the "aggressor."

Physical Bullying Hurting a person's body or their possessions.

School Climate The quality, character, social atmosphere, and 'feel' of the school, mostly exhibited by patterns of behavior and interactions among and between students and school personnel.

Social Bullying Spreading rumors to hurt someone's reputation and/or excluding them from being part of a social group. Also referred to as covert or relational bullying.

Social Networking Sites Online services that bring together people by organizing them around a common interest and providing an interactive environment of photos, blogs, user profiles, and messaging systems. Examples include Facebook and Instagram.

Stereotype An oversimplified generalization about a person or group of people without regard for individual differences. Even seemingly positive stereotypes that link a person or group to a specific positive trait can have negative consequences.

Texting Sending a short message via phone.

Threat Making a statement of taking an action that implies or suggests harm to someone else

Verbal Bullying Saying and/or writing hurtful and mean things.

Victim The person who is on the receiving end of social cruelty. Also known as the "target."

Wireless Device Electronic devices that can access the Internet without being physically attached by a cable or data line.

References

Anti-Defamation League. (2014). *What is weight bias?* Retrieved from https://www.adl.org/sites/default/files/documents/assets/pdf/education-outreach/what-is-weight-bias.pdf

Cyberbullying Research Center. (2017). *Glossary*. Retrieved from https://cyberbullying.org/glossary

Hinduja, S., & Patchin, J. W. (2009). *Bullying beyond the schoolyard: Preventing and responding to cyberbullying.* Thousand oaks, CA: Corwin Press.

Nansel, T. R., Overpeck, M., Pilla, R. S., Ruan, W. J., Simons-Morton, B., & Scheidt, P. (2001). Bullying behaviors among US youth: Prevalence and association with psychosocial development. *JAMA: Journal of the American Medical Association, 285*(16), 2094–2100.

National Center Against Bullying. (2017). *Types of bullying*. Retrived from https://www.ncab.org.au/bullying-advice/bullying-for-parents/types-of-bullying/

Shetgiri, R. (2013). Bullying and victimization among children. *JAMAL: Journal of the American Medical Association, 60*(1), 33–51.

U.S. Equal Employment Opportunity Commission. (2017). *Harassment*. Retrieved from https://www.eeoc.gov/laws/types/harassment.cfm

CHAPTER 4

The Little Rascals
Memorable Movie Bullies

Those teachers above the age of forty reading this will probably remember the terror in the eyes of Spanky, Alfalfa, and the rest of Our Gang when they were confronted by Butch and Woim, the neighborhood bully and his henchman on the streets of Greenpoint. The presence of Butch and Woim normalized the mediated movie/TV bully. Their tactics of torture were renowned and left many a young viewer trembling in fear. Their horrible antics were revived in the 1994 reboot. Even after forty years, Alfalfa and Butch were still competing for Darla's attention.

The Little Rascals
(Universal Pictures, 1994)
11:10–12:40

The mediated bully has taken several forms. In some ways, the image created a false expectation of what bullies "look" like and how they operate. Perhaps children imagine that bullies act the way they've seen them on the silver screen and, in so doing, have limited the possibilities of teachers intervening. This chapter gives an overview of the popular bully archetypes in the movies.

Anti-Social Behaviors

The most popular bully image is that of the hostile antisocial. This is the ne'er do well, aggressive, "bad kid" in school. He often displayed negative behaviors and was disruptive in class, Hostile and rude, the antisocial bully picked on boys and girls on the playground, in the locker rooms, and in the cafeterias. He was a deviant, a juvenile delinquent, and was defiant to his teachers and other authorities.

The image that comes to mind is Sid from *Toy Story*. Sid is Andy's neighbor and when we see him, he is sporting a skull and crossbones on his T-shirt—perhaps signaling his negative character as the green Mr. Yuck sticker told kids to stay away from household chemicals. Sid exploded toys with fireworks and disfigures toys. When he is first introduced, the toys cringe at his appearance:

Slinky Dog:	"It's Sid!"
Rex:	"I thought he was at summer camp!"
Hamm:	"They must have kicked him out early this year."

Falling in the same character type as "Psycho Sid" is Troy McGinty from the *Max Keeble* movies. Early in *Max Keeble's Big Move,* Troy (Noel Fisher) stands on a bench in the school's hallway. He announces his latest target to bully by wearing the name on his t-shirt. He unzips his jacket to reveal "Freak with Robe." The scene shifts to the gym class of Robe (Josh Peck) running laps. Robe enters the locker room, but Troy grabs him saying, "Hello, freak." In the next scene several students are watching, pointing, and laughing as Troy has stuffed Robe into a glass trophy case. Max (Alex Linz) releases him just before Robe vomits. The scene shifts to Dobbs (Orlando Brown) charging a male student to use the urinal. Troy busts in dragging Max and he asks Dobbs "How much for a swirlie?" Dobbs answers, "No charge" and opens a stall door.

The antisocial has a long history. This is revealed in *Max Keeble* when Marley (Jordan Mahome) is dictating the school's history of bullying. He admits "Curtis Junior High has a long and fascinating history of colorful bullies." He describes, "In 1985, Tomato-face Callahan. He'd walk right up and shove a tomato in your face. 1991, Wedgie Jackson. He invented the world wide wedge. Which brings us to this year. Troy McGinty." The scene shifts to Troy, clad in all black, chains, and boots. Marley continues, "Word is, he's gonna pound on a different kid every day. And he's devised his own special way of letting the world know who he's coming after." Troy unzips his jacket to show Max Keeble's name and the growd gasps.

Later, Troy has announced that Max Keebler will be his "First victim of the year—a big honor." In a voice-over, Max narrates his history with Troy: "You know the guy you hung out with when you were little, but as you got older you went in opposite directions? Well, Troy McGinty wasn't always a bully. I remember when he came to my fourth birthday. The theme was "MacGoogles the Frog." The scene cuts to a televised image of MacGoogles and a younger Troy crying "I don't like MacGoogles!" The other kids at the party call Troy a "scaredy cat" when he flinches when Max's dad enters dressed in a MacGoogles costume. Fast forward to Troy carrying Max down the hallway and outside to a mud puddle where he throws Max. Two other students excitedly take a picture before Troy dumps a load of sawdust on Max. Troy finishes by tossing Max in the dumpster.

Another antisocial exemplar is Buddy Revell from *Three O'Clock High.* Buddy's reputation preceded him long before he made an appearance in the film. He is reputed to have done very bad things at his previous schools and Jerry Mitchell (Casey Siemaszko) is assigned to write a profile piece on Buddy for the school newspaper. Jerry encounters Buddy as Jerry stands at the urinal [14:09–18:31] when he realizes that Buddy is standing next to him. Jerry tries to make introductions, but Buddy interrupts, "If you're a fag…" Jerry explains that he works for the school newspaper and has been tasked to write a piece on Buddy being the new kid at school. Jerry mistakenly touches Buddy's

THE LITTLE RASCALS

shoulder—a definite no-no! Buddy physically assaults Jerry. Buddy argues that Jerry can "Take that newspaper of yours and wipe your dick off with it." Buddy threatens that he must work off his anger by fighting Jerry at 3:00. He warns, "You try and run, I'm gonna track you down. You go to a teacher, it's only gonna get worse. You sneak home, I'm gonna be under your bed." The scene ends as Buddy leaves the bathroom leaving Jerry a little shell-shocked. Later, Jerry follows Buddy into the gymnasium and pleads with him to call off the fight. Jerry offers Buddy $350 to call off the fight. Buddy accepts saying, "You'll live." Buddy calls Jerry a "pussy" for not even trying to fight and questions "How does that feel?" as he exits the gym [1:08:56–1:11:09].

Perhaps the most memorable of the antisocial types was Biff Tannen of the *Back to the Future* series. Biff was the antagonist to Marty McFly and to his father George. Actually, Biff started bullying George when they were in high school in the 1950s and his antics continued into adulthood. By the time Marty (Michael J. Fox) went back in time, Biff practically owned George (Crispin Glover).

Biff's Bullying Scenes across the Back to the Future Trilogy

Back to the Future 38:40–41:06
Back to the Future Part 2 12:43–21:15
Back to the Future Part 3 30:03–35:05, 56:58–1:02:15

Biff is not to be overshadowed, but he is rivaled. He is rivaled for antisocial supremacy by Moody (Matt Dillon) in 1980s classic *My Bodyguard*. Belying his antisocial status, Moody was charismatic in his deviance. He fancied himself a ladies' man and while his teachers were aware of his no-goodness, he was still able to win them over with his charm.

Even if it was forced, Moody's peers respected him. In fact, Moody enters the classroom to much fanfare [13:26–17:21] When the teacher asks him to find a seat, Moody looks at Clifford (Chris Makepeace) and declares "This sucker swiped it from me." Chris defends, "I was here first!" Moody returns, "Bullshit!" The teacher continues to take attendance. When she gets to Clifford's name, she asks for the correct pronunciation. He says it's "Peach." Moody announces, "I knew he was a fruit." Moody desires to be called "Big M"; Clifford remarks, "Is that 'B.M.' for short?" Sensing Moody's ire, Reissman (Tom Rielly) adds, "You've got nerve, even if you're not gonna live long." Moody tells Clifford, "You and me, we're gonna have a little talk after school." In a later class, Reissman tells

Clifford, "You know that was so dumb what you said to Moody this morning. I never saw anybody put him down before. I hope you get away with it...Don't let him catch you in the halls alone, or on the stairs either. Or especially in the bathrooms. I never go to the bathroom here, if I can help it. They say one kid got thrown out a window last year. He's a vegetable now. Another guy had his eye kicked out. Total gross-out." Clifford wonders if Moody was responsible for hurting the other kid. Reissman defends, "I'm not saying he did, and I'm not saying he didn't. But from my point of view, you're better off paying him protection money." Reissman explains how Moody takes kids lunch money, so he brings his lunch to school. "Now he claims he's gonna take my bus fare." Clifford suggests not allowing Moody to get away with it, but Reismman declares, "I know, but I'm kind of addicted to breathing."

Clifford channels Moody's ire quickly. That same day [18:40–22:23], Clifford is walking down the hall after school when he is delivered by a couple young men to Moody in the boys' bathroom. Moody is currently involved with harassing a different boy and demanding that boy to give him a dollar every day. Moody slings wet wads of toilet paper at Clifford's head. Moody scoops a cup of filth from the toilet and demands Clifford eat it. Clifford throws the contents in Moody's face and flees the bathroom.

The antisocial bully is a mainstay in popular movie types, Newbies and nerds should beware as they were most often the targets of the antisocial bully type.

Scut Farkus is another. With his yellow eyes, Scut (Zack Ward) antagonized the neighborhood in *A Christmas Story* (1983). Ralphie (Peter Billingsley) and his friends are walking home from school and discussing the day's excitement. Soon, they hear the familiar laugh of Scut Farkus, their feared nemesis [21:50–23:59]. After he pushes Randy (Ian Petrella) down, he roars and scares Ralphie and crew, who run in the opposite direction. They are scared back by Grover Dill, "Farkus' crummy little toady. Mean. Rotten. His lips curled over his green teeth." Farkus grabs Schwartz and wrenches his arm behind him until Scwartz cries out "Uncle!" Ralph (voiced as an adult) narrates "In our world, you were either a bully, a toady, or one of the nameless rabble of victims." The scene ends after the boys run away and the bullies walk in a separate direction.

Films of the 1980s seemed to champion the antisocial type of bully. Another example of the type can be found in Stephen King's *Stand by Me* (1986). Gordie (Wil Wheaton) and Chris (River Phoenix) encounter Ace (Kiefer Sutherland) and Eyeball (Bradley Gregg) outside a department store. Chris calls. Ace a "real asshole" after Ace steals Gordie's hat. Ace offers "the opportunity of taking it back" threatening to burn Chris with a lit cigarette. Once Chris apologizes," Ace responds, "Now I feel a whole lot better about this. How about you?" [12:38–13:45].

Most of the antisocial bullying behaviors seem to not have a cause—these kids bully because they're "bad dudes." At least one example, however, seemed to be trained to act that way. Billy Zabka played Johnny in *The Karate Kid* (1984). Johnny was a karate star who paraded about town with his friends and beating up other kids at will. Johnny was trained to be an asshole by his sensei, his teacher, Kreese (Martin Kove). In a training session, Kreese challenges his students to have "no mercy" on their opponents.

For most of the film, Johnny sees Daniel (Ralph Macchio) as his opponent for the love/attention of Ali (Elisabeth Shue), Johnny's ex-girlfriend. One evening [11:20–14:20], Ali and Daniel are playing on the beach when Johnny and his friends approach on their motorcycles. Johnny harasses Ali and Daniel attempts to stand in for her, but Johnny beats him up and leaves him lying in the sand.

Later, Daniel (Ralph Macchio) is riding his bike alone at night [25:19–26:08]. He notices Johnny and friends riding their motorcycles towards him. The boys begin to taunt: "Looking for a shortcut back to Newark, Daniel?" Johnny adds, "No, he wants to learn karate. Here's your first lesson: How to take a fall. Don't think about the pain." They push Daniel and cause him to fall down a nearby hill.

Zabka unfortunately was typecast into similar roles throughout the late 1980s and early 1990s. In *Just One of the Guys* (1985), Zabka plays Greg Toler whose sole mission seemed to be to show what he was made of. He delights in torturing freshmen and new kids. This film follows Terry Griffith (Joyce Hyser) who masquerades as a male to earn a journalism award. It's Terry's first day at school in her new identity as a boy and as she approaches the doors, she notices Greg demonstrating weight lifting strategies to his friends. Greg tells them "Once you're into power-blitzing, doing super sets is like jerking off. The key is to work out every possible minute. Like say you don't have any weights. You use freshmen." He demonstrates on a passing freshman [17:46–20:05]. Terry uncomfortably laughs along until Greg wonders why he is there. Terry admits, "I'm new here." Greg remarks, "Just what we need—another pussy." Terry insults Greg and he continues his strength demonstration: "Another good exercise for upper body strength—the pussy toss for distance." Greg tosses Terry into the bushes. Later in the cafeteria, showing off his strength and athleticism, Greg disrupts a table of outcasts' lunch by lifting their table while they eat. When that fails to get a rise out of them, he lifts their bench until several fall off [23:13–23:45].

In *Welcome to the Dollhouse*, Brandon (Brendon Sexton) is a traditional antisocial bully who threatens to rape Dawn Weiner (Heather Matarazzo) when she intervenes on Brandon while he is bullying another boy. Dawn spends the day in fear awaiting Brendan's 3:00 promise [1:51–5:08].

The Pack of Bullies

True to its name, the antisocial type often works alone. Yet, bullying, as pointed out by consultant Dan Olweus, happens within a social network. Olweus (1994) called this the bullying circle. He identifies that there is a lead bully and several bystanders—some of whom are involved and support the bullying and some who are not. In the movies, however, bullies act in concert with each other in a sort of pack like wolves. Yes, there is an Alpha wolf, but the bully group is powerful and prey upon the weak and (socially) infirmed.

As the phrase goes "there is strength in numbers," the lead bully finds strength in the group. The gang of bullies are a common movie trope. In the movie titled *2:37* (so named as at 2:37, a student committed suicide in the school bathroom). The day is played out in the lives of six students as the story is told. In a short scene early in the film [18:00–19:15] Luke is greeted in the school hallway by his friends. He asks what transpired at the party they attended after he left. Luke explains, "I was fuckin' gone, man." His friend agreed, "You were fucked." Luke tells the story how while he was in the bathroom, Ben tapped him on the shoulder. Luke turns around and just piss[ed] all over this guy. "You fucking pissed all over him, replied one of the boys? What did Ben do?" Luke replies, "What could he do man? He was covered in piss." Just then, the boys sight Sean who is kneeling at his locker. The three circle around him and begin to taunt. "Hey Seany! How's it going, buddy? You'd get fucking shit on your dick?" They all laugh while the ribbing continues, "Hey, Sean, do you like taking it or giving it, huh?" They mimic sexual noises and acts. One of the boys adds, "Hey, come on, give us a kiss." Sean yells, "Get the fuck off me!" Luke questions, "We're not good enough for you, Seany?" Sean stares at each of them. As he walks off, he declares, "You're fucking pathetic." One of the boys defends, "You fucking cock jockey!" The scene ends as Melody walks in and kisses her boyfriend.

The gang mentality is further explicated in the film *Dodgeball: A True Underdog Story* (2004) [21:57–24:27]. The scene opens on an educational film discussing the history and rules of the game of dodgeball. Patches O'Houlihan (Hank Azaria) enters to give strategies on winning the game. "But remember, dodgeball is a sport of violence, exclusion, and degradation. So, when you're picking players in gym class, remember to pick the bigger, stronger kids for your team. That way, you can all gang up on the weaker ones." The scene ends as Patches reviews the five D's of Dodgeball: duck, dodge, dip, dive, and dodge.

In 2010's *Let Me In* Owen (Kodi Smit McPhee) is in the locker room getting his book bag when Kenny (Dylan Minnette) calls him a little girl [15:58–17:21]. Owen tries to escape him, but is blocked by Kenny's friends. Kenny repeatedly snaps his towel in Owen's face. Kenny suggests, "That's why he won't go swimming. He doesn't want everyone to see what a little fucking girl he is." When Owen tries to run away again, the boys pin him down while Kenny gives Owen a wedgie. Owen repeatedly yells for the boys to stop, but they only stop when they see that Owen has "pissed himself." One of the boys kicks Owen and shouts "Jesus Christ, fucking freak!" The boys depart the locker room cheering that "Owen pissed himself."

The gang is at it again in the 2003 film *Radio* about a mentally challenged man named Radio who assists a high school football coach (played by Ed Harris). In a scene towards the middle of the film [1:11:12–1:14:28], Radio (Cuba Gooding, Jr.) is cleaning up in the coach's office when several other boys tell him that Coach Dalrymple needs help in the girls' locker room. Radio complies as not to disappoint. Radio goes into the locker room and several girls scream. Radio runs out whimpering, "Bad Radio. Bad Radio." Later, Radio refuses to tell on the boys who goaded him.

In a ridiculous scene in the 2008 film *Stepbrothers* [44:12–45:19], the gang bullying motif is portrayed when Dale (John C. Reilly) and Brennan (Will Ferrell) are walking down the street and are confronted by Chris Gardocki (Logan Manus) and a group of other children. Chris states, "Let's make him lick dog shit." Chris calls Dale a "fag-stick" and wonders if Brennan is his "butty buddy." One child threatens, "If you don't come over here and lick that white dog shit, I'm gonna plow into your nose with my fist." Brennan responds, "I'm not licking any white dog shit, but Dale enters, "I'll lick the shit if you leave us alone." Brennan adds, "Dale, you're not licking dog shit okay? They're kids." The kids beat on the men and the scene ends when Brennan scream after licking the white turd.

A pack of kids as the bullies is portrayed shortly after the opening credits [0:50–4:40] of the film *The Benchwarmers*, where three socially inept young children are playing baseball in the local park when members of the organized little league team try to force them off the diamond. One of the young kids argues that the team's practice does not start until 4:30; the team leader states "We want to have a practice before the practice." A girl who was with the original group suggests they all play together when an older boy retorts "No, because you suck. Why don't you go home and build your science projects." The oldest boy pushes the other boy down, and while another team member holds him, the oldest nearly sits on the boy's face and gives him some "beef stew" (he farted just above his nose). The young boy is rescued when an adult named Gus (played by Rob Schneider) chases the older boys away. In tears, the young boy tells Gus, "It actually didn't taste as bad as you'd think" and runs away. Gus ponders, "Why do kids have to be so fricking cruel?"

Bullying by the "In Crowd"

In movies, the gang of bullies trope is often carried out by members of the "in crowd" of popular kids. They rule the school hallways and make life hell for the social outcasts and misfits. The "in crowd" is often made up of the most athletic, most beautiful, and most popular kids in the high school. Their actions dictate how others are "supposed" to dress, to behave, to think, and to feel about certain aspects of teen life. What they say goes and insolence is not accepted or tolerated—the consequences are often social isolation or exclusion. The "in crowd" owns the school and they are frequently depicted walking as a triumphant force stretching across the hallways. The website TV Tropes refers to this as the Power Walk (TVTropes, 2018). The walk includes characters shoulder to shoulder, looking cool, determinedly as they walk towards the camera. The walk is a tool used to display unity among the social group. Examples can be seen in *Love Don't Cost a Thing* [9:39–11:33]; *You Again* [0:22–1:48]; and *Read It and Weep* [3:50–5:20].

This is where most female bullies in film pop up. The most popular being Regina George, the Queen Bee from *Mean Girls*. Rachel McAdams plays Regina in this 2004 classic and she rules the school with fierce expectations. She leads The Plastics, defined by outcast Damien (Daniel Franzese) as "teen royalty." Damien contends, "If North Shore [their high school] was *Us Weekly*, they would always be on the cover." Damien and Janis (Lizzy Caplan) explain the identities of each of The Plastics to Cady (Lindsay Lohan), the new student. Janis describes "And evil takes a human form in Regina George. Don't be fooled, because she may seem like your typical selfish, back-stabbing, slut-faced ho bag. But in reality, she is so much more than that." Damien interrupts, "She is the queen bee. The star. Those other two are just her workers." Janis continues, "How do I even begin to explain Regina George?" A montage of other students—most of whom would be Regina's targets describe Regina as "flawless" and cite her expensive belongings and high brow activities endorsing her status.

Later, Cady is invited to join The Plastics for lunch [13:37–15:20]. Cady (Lindsay Lohan) narrates "Eating lunch with the Plastics was like leaving the actual world and entering 'Girl World.' And Girl World had a lot of rules." Gretchen (Lacey Chabert) begins the list of rules. After detailing the rules, Gretchen adds, "Now, if you break any of these rules, you can't sit with us at lunch. I mean, not just you. Like, any of us." Gretchen further explains rules about clothing styles and dating. "Ex-boyfriends are just off-limits to friends. I mean, that's just, like, the rules of feminism." Regina keeps a "burn book" where The Plastics write mean or embarrassing comments about other students. Regina mistreats everyone *including* those she calls friends even her mom.

She dictates who people date and for how long. Janis calls her a "life ruiner" when she steals Cady's love interest. Janis concocts a plan to take down Regina. "Regina George is an evil dictator. Now, how do you overthrow a dictator? You cut off her resources. Regina would be nothing without her high-status man candy, technically good physique, and ignorant band of loyal followers."

Similar to Regina George, Priscilla (Jaime Pressly) in *Not Another Teen Movie* a 2001 spoof on the high school movie genre, is a teen mean queen. Her target in the film is Janey (Chyler Leigh). One evening [43:21–44:50], Janey stands on a balcony at a party and jumps into the pool. When she gets out of the pool, Priscilla (Jaime Pressly) and her friends approach Janey and question her presence at the party. Priscilla argues, "Look, you may have lost those glasses and that ponytail thing you do, but to everyone that matters, you're still a loser." Priscilla pours a bottle of water on Janey and challenges her not to cry. Janey runs away crying.

Social exclusion is a regular part of bullying in film perpetrated by girls. In *Odd Girl Out* (2005), isolation is the consequence of having a romantic crush on the popular girl's love interest. Starring Alexa PenVega as Vanessa, *Odd Girl Out* is true to its name. In a scene (beginning at 17:41 and ending at 19:10), A group of girls are seated in the cafeteria. Tiffany (Alicia Morton)is telling a story, "Her clothes were hideous. And I was looking at her hair style; it was horrible, and I was, like, 'Who does your hair, the gardener?'" Soon, Vanessa (Alexa PenaVega) approaches and tries to sit down bur Nikki blocks her. "Oh, come on, Nik, I know you have an SUV for an ass, but just park it in one spot." Nikki deflects, "There's plenty of room over there." Tiffany calls Vanessa a "slut." The scene ends when Vanessa goes to another table. Later, Vanessa (Alexa PenaVega) has been ostracized to the "losers' table" in the cafeteria. She has been befriended by Emily (Shari Perry) who tells her she missed the action in English class. Emily tells Vanessa, "You know why they keep dogging you? They do it because they know it gets to you. I call them the 'white tornadoes' because they destroy whatever's in their path." Soon, another female student brings over a laptop showing a meme of Vanessa eating and getting fatter while onlookers laugh. Later, Vanessa approaches Tony (Chad Biagini) at his locker and he shuns her [23:06–25:45].

Being a part of the "in crowd" in film has its perks. Being a part of the outcasts is no walk in the park. You're kept out of the best parties; you're ignored, and in *Love Don't Cost a Thing*, the urban reboot of the 80s hit film *Can't Buy Me Love*, the misfits are prohibited from walking down certain corridors in school [9:39–11:33]. Alvin (Nick Cannon) and his friends desire to be cool enough to be able to walk down the popular kids' hallway. They realize they do not have the social capital to do so because they are "invisible" to the popular crowd.

Kenneth (Kal Penn) states, "in that community, we're immigrants without green cards." Fed up with being an outcast, Walter (Kenan Thompson) decides to walk down the hallway; he is immediately rebuffed. Walter tries to prove his coolness by revealing the label of his jeans. Ted (Al Thompson) pushes him against a locker and asks, "Is that the gay surrender? You a homo thug?" He threatens Walter with physical violence. The scene ends as Al and friends carry Walter away.

One of the most memorable films related to bullying by the in-crowd is Stephen King's *Carrie* (1976). Carrie (played by Sissy Spacek) lives a sheltered life with her very religious mother, and when she experiences her period for the first time in the gym shower, which draws the furor of the popular kids, led by Nancy (Chris Hargensen). In this opening scene [3:49–6:09], Carrie White is taking a shower when she sees blood pouring down her legs. She panics and runs naked from the shower screaming for assistance from other students. The girls laugh and hang tampons and throw maxipads at her taunting "Plug it up!" Carrie's teacher intervenes and tries to calm Carrie down.

Later, in the infamous prom scene [1:10:09–1:19:15], Nancy targets Carrie and Tommy (William Katt). Carrie and Tommy have just been elected king and queen of the prom. They approach the stage to the adulation of many at the prom. They are unaware that Nancy, Cindy and others have plotted to embarrass her by spilling pig's blood on the couple. The bucket hits Tommy in the head and knocks him unconscious. Using her telekinetic powers, Carrie annihilates the students as they run from the building.

These three archetypes cover the gamut of bullying in film. While males predominantly are represented in the antisocial and gang of bullies archetypes and women in "in crowd" category, it is important to recognize the categories are not exclusive in real life. These archetypes in popular film leave lasting images and it is necessary to understand their impact on viewers. Archetypes are not easily dismissed and they are often seen without intent of harm. Jungian psychology suggests archetypes are deeply held images which influence psychological development and personal experience, intersect with culture, and are useful as the mechanism for balance to make sure all is "right" with the world around us (Hockley, 2007). Bully archetypes in film support the notion of the normativity (Solebello & Elliot, 2011) of bullying in American thought and culture.

CHAPTER 5

See No Evil, Hear No Evil
Changing Bystander Attitudes

One of the most significant ways to create an anti-bullying culture is to challenge the bystander effect. A bystander, according to national collegiate speaker, Mike Dilbeck, is "someone who 'stands by' when they see or hear about a problem situation, even though they may find it to be problematic." Bullying rarely happens in private, and these situations are commonly witnessed by a group of others.

Within the Olweus bullying circle, the bystanders play various roles. Some bystanders encourage the bully through instigation, some by laughing and cheering (although not all those who laugh laugh because they are happy about the bullying), some actively participate once the bullying begins, still other bystanders passively accept what is happening [many feel powerless to intervene].

That inability to intervene is at the heart of the "bystander effect" (Gini, Pozzoli, Borghi, & Franzoni, 2008). The bystander effect is the impact on individuals, groups, and society of people being bystanders and not intervening. Bystanders often fall victim to the attitude that curing the culture is not their responsibility, but should be done by someone else. Bystanders often fail to act because of several barriers: (a) social influence (others are not doing anything so there must not be a problem, (b) fear of embarrassment (to self or others), (c) diffusion of responsibility (assuming someone else will do something, (d) fear of retaliation (of physical or emotional harm), or (e) pluralistic ignorance (everyone does it) or (I'm the only one who thinks this way).

The bystander effect is an off-shoot from the idea of "group think" whereby the presence of others inhibits the desire to help exponentially. The more people there are, the less likely that anyone will intervene. We are more likely to intervene when we're a part of a cohesive group with shared norms and values about intervening. This may be the theory behind the Transportation Security Administration (TSA) slogan "If you see something, say something." There is safety in numbers; many school districts adopt community rules regarding bullying behaviors in an attempt to create school cultures where individuals feel safe and supported to intervene and end bullying. Adoption of bully-free "zones" are consistent with this culture shift (Rowan, 2007; Spurling, 2004).

Putting an end to bullying may begin and end with empowering bystanders to intervene by doing something to actively stop the bullying behavior or to at least get help from an authority or peer. We must eschew schadenfreude and interrupt the maltreatment of others (Leach, Spears, & Doosje, 2003). Empowering bystanders requires more than just saying "Speak up!" but requires a paradigmatic shift where individual youth can drown out the cacophony of voices that co-sign bullying behavior overtly or through silence. It is not uncommon for bystanders to experience feelings of fear, discomfort, guilt and helplessness. The associated and attributed fears are related to:

> *The Final*
> (Agora Entertainment, 2010)
> 1:25:17–1:27:10
>
> *The Perks of Being a Wallflower*
> (Summit Entertainment, 2012)
> 1:09:30–1:14:00

- Association with the victim and fear of retribution by the bully (Smith & Sharp, 2002);
- Being labeled a "snitch" or "tattle tale" (Shapiro & Vote, 2014);
- Feelings of guilt for not helping (Wilson, Droždek, & Turkovic, 2006);
- The pressure to join in (Pozzoli & Gini, 2010);
- Lack of safety (Coloroso, 2004).

Bystander behavior changes from elementary school through upper grades. Elementary-aged children tend to be more authority driven and will tell the teacher. Middles schoolers are much more socially aware and are more likely to be concerned about feeling "different" and fearing reprisal. High school kids may fight, may ignore, and are more likely to intervene or show disapproval.

> *A Lesson on the Effects of Bystanders*
> https://www.boystownpress.org/samplePDFs/48-014_NoRoomforBulliesLessonPlans.pdf

Changing bystander behavior necessitates empowering onlookers and witnesses to "shift from passively watching bullying to actively defending targets" (Davis & Davis, 2007, p. 75). The following quote attributed to Martin Niemöller is a great example of bystander behavior and its ramifications:

> *First they came for the Socialists, and I did not speak out—*
> *Because I was not a Socialist.*
> *Then they came for the Trade Unionists, and I did not speak out—*
> *Because I was not a Trade Unionist.*
> *Then they came for the Jews, and I did not speak out—*
> *Because I was not a Jew.*
> *Then they came for me—and there was no one left to speak for me.*
> https://www.ushmm.org/wlc/en/article.php?ModuleId=10007392

References

Coloroso, B. (2004). *The bully, the bullied and the bystander.* New York, NY: HarperCollins.

Davis, S., & Davis, J. (2007). *Empowering bystanders in bullying prevention: Grades K-8.* Champaign, IL: Research Press.

Gini, G., Pozzoli, T., Borghi, F., & Franzoni, L. (2008). The role of bystanders in students' perception of bullying and sense of safety. *Journal of School Psychology, 46*(6), 617–638.

Leach, C. W., Spears, R., Branscombe, N. R., & Doosje, B. (2003). Malicious pleasure: Schadenfreude at the suffering of another group. *Journal of Personality and Social Psychology, 84*(5), 932.

Pozzoli, T., & Gini, G. (2010). Active defending and passive bystanding behavior in bullying: The role of personal characteristics and perceived peer pressure. *Journal of Abnormal Child Psychology, 38*(6), 815–827.

Rowan, L. O. (2007). Making classrooms bully-free zones: Practical suggestions for educators. *Kappa Delta Pi Record, 43*(4), 182–185.

Shapiro, O., & Vote, S. (2014). *Bullying and me: Schoolyard stories.* New York, NY: Open Road Media.

Smith, P. K., & Sharp, S. (2002). The problem of school bullying. In P. K. Smith & S. Sharp (Eds.), *School Bullying: Insights and perspectives.* London & New York, NY: Routledge.

Spurling, R. A. (2004). *The bully-free school zone character education program: A study of impact on five Western North Carolina middle schools.* East Tennessee, TN: East Tennessee State University Dissertation Research.

TVTropes. (2018, August 1). *Power walk.* Retrieved from https://tvtropes.org/pmwiki/pmwiki.php/Main/PowerWalk

Wilson, J. P., Drožđek, B., & Turkovic, S. (2006). Posttraumatic shame and guilt. *Trauma, Violence, & Abuse, 7*(2), 122–141.

CHAPTER 6

Dangerous Minds
Prevailing Attitudes about Bullying Culture

Bullying has been an issue for school children that often goes unreported. Limber and Small (2003) found that "historically, bullying among school children has not been a topic of significant public concern" (p. 445). Throughout history people felt that bullying was a normal part of school culture, and has been overlooked. Hart (2004) stated "until recent years, bullying was viewed by most parents and educators as a typical part of growing up" (p. 1115). The notion that bullying was a common aspect of growing up comes from three core beliefs: (1) assertive beliefs; e.g., children would not be bullied or picked on if they would stand up for themselves; (2) bullying is normative behavior that helps children learn social norms; and (3) avoidant beliefs; e.g., children would not be bullied or picked on if they avoided mean kids (Kochenderfer-Ladd & Pelletier, 2008. These beliefs are based on how many people viewed and continue to view bullying in our society. Think back to when you were growing up. How many of you heard things like "oh, that's just kids being kids," "you have to toughen up," and you just have to ignore them. This way of thinking has caused bullying to become so common in our schools and brushed off. Thanks to more research and attention on the issue, we know that bullying is not only an issue for students but an issue for school teachers and the school environment.

A Dear Colleague letter for the U.S. Department of Education stated "bullying fosters a climate of fear and disrespect that can seriously impair the physical and psychological health of its victims and create conditions that negatively affect learning, thereby undermining the ability of students to achieve their full potential" (Ali, 2010, p. 1). Despite these assertions, Brown (2008) found that "more than 5.7 million teens in the United States are estimated to be a bully, a target of bullying, or both" (p. 44). Bullying is a concern because it can be abusive and humiliating, as well as destructive (Wight, 2008). Despite the damaging impact of bullying, the incidents continue to occur in schools. The question that arises is what makes a student want to bully another student.

Odd Girl Out
(Jaffe/Braunstein Films, 2005)
36:52–38:22

The reasons for bullying vary from person to person and situation. Bullies pick their targets to make themselves look and/or feel tough and in control.

DANGEROUS MINDS

Bullies target people because they do not like them, or they look for a reaction from others. Often times bullies believe that by targeting others students it will improve their social status, i.e. popularity in the school (Rettner, 2104).

Bullying someone who is different begins with characteristics that are visibly noticeable. The characteristics can range from weight, height, a disability, clothing or shoes, ethnicity and students who identify or perceived as LGBT (Bullyingnoway, 2017). Students may target those that are different because they are lead to believe that it is fun to make fun of those people. In school, students mimic what they see on social media watch on Netflix and what they see in movies.

In movies, there are many examples where characters are bullied because of their race or the way they look. One example comes from the movie *The Final*. In an early scene [8:34–9:54], Ravi (Vincent Silochan) is in the bathroom putting batteries in his camera when Bernard (Daniel Ross Owens) and Riggs (Preston Flagg) enter. Bernard questions, "What do we have here, son, huh? If it isn't the *Slumdog Millionaire*." Riggs forms a pistol with his hands and points it at Ravi. "What's up Bin Laden?" Ravi responds, "I'm Indian, not Arab." Before placing Ravi in a headlock, he takes Ravi's camera and suggests Ravi is "doing a little recon for his terrorist cell." Riggs slams Ravi's camera to the ground in a mock football play, "Cause I felt like it." Dane (Marc Donato) walks in looking for Ravi. Dane asks "Did you guys break his camera?" Riggs admits, "Yeah, I did. I busted it." Grabbing Dane by the throat, he continues, "The question is, what the fuck are you gonna do about it, huh?" Riggs challenges Dane to a fight, but Dane admits he can't beat Riggs. Riggs suggests, it's "'Cause you're a coward." Riggs argues, "You know why it is that I do what I do to you? Do you know? I do it because I know that you can't stop me?" Riggs tells Bernard "Let's leave these pussies." Dane puts a reassuring hand on Ravi and suggests "Soon."

After showing this clip to your students, some follow-up questions can help engage students in a healthy discussion about differences.

Possible Questions to Ask Students

1. What makes Riggs feel the need to refer to Ravi as Bin Laden?
2. How do you think Ravi feels in this scene?
3. What message do you take away from this scene?
4. If you had a chance to ask any of the characters a question, what would it be?
5. What would your parent (s) say after viewing this? Your best friend? Your teacher?

Another movie scene focuses on a young man being teased based on his weight. In a scene from *Fat Boy Chronicles* [20:03–24:36], Jimmy Winterpock (Christopher Rivera) is changing in the locker room following gym class when Robb (Cole Carson) begins to call him "stupid" claiming "Don't you know? This is our spot." Jimmy tries to leave but is blocked. "Robb continues to berate him. "Hey cutie. Is this your locker room?" When another student approaches, Robb points at Jimmy's chest. "Look at that chest. It's bigger than Whitney's [Robb's girlfriend]. So, are you like a D-cup?" The coach interrupts and tells the boys to hurry up. After the coach leaves, Robb gathers the other students around, "Hey guys. I was thinking maybe we should change our mascot to the Big Round Blueberries." Robb and friends leave the locker room.

Central Intelligence
(New Line Cinema, 2016)
1:03–5:13

The film clip focused on the issue of bullying and humiliation based on weight. In class you can use some of the questions below to help facilitate a discussion about bullying and body image.

Possible Questions to Ask Students

1. How do you think Jimmy felt?
2. Where do you see people being targeted because of their weight (school, home, television, social media)
3. Should Jimmy tell Coach Robb about the situation?
4. Is bullying based on a weight an issue at your school?
   a. In your community?
   b. In media?

These clips were two examples among many that demonstrate how bullying behavior is displayed on the big screen. Oftentimes, these scenes are shown in a comedic form. No matter how many ways bullying behavior is seen by students, it important to note that bullying is a concern for all students. No matter if the student is seen as popular or the outsider in school, all students can be impacted by bullying. Despite the different ways students are exposed to bullying behavior, school teachers and administrators and parents can take proactive steps to help address the issue of bullying. Teachers can start by creating and maintaining a classroom that is welcoming to all students. Be sure to display encouraging postings and affirmations (Miller, 2009). Where appropriate, teachers should feel comfortable integrating discussions of bullying inside the classroom. The discussion can help students know that teachers and administrators are there if they need help (Miller, 2009). Students should know who to go to see to report bullying incidents. Schools should educate all students about bullying with facts and dispel the myths about bullying (Miller, 2009). School Districts need to conduct a survey to get the perception of bullying within their school. Ensure that information is available regarding the school policy on bullying. Parents play a vital role in addressing bullying as well. Parents should talk to their children about their interaction with other peers at school. It strongly encouraged that parents attend parent-teacher conference and be involved in the Parent Teacher Association in order to stay up-to-date on school policies.

Drillbit Taylor
(20th Century Fox, 2004)
1:17:22–1:19:01

References

Ali, R. (2010, October 26). *Dear colleague letter: Harassment and bullying.* Retrieved from http://www2.ed.gov/about/offices/list/ocr/letters/colleague-201010.pdf

Bullyingnoway. (2017). *Diversity and bullying.* Retrieved from https://bullyingnoway.gov.au/UnderstandingBullying/WhyDoesBullyingHappen/Pages/Diversity-and-bullying.aspx

Hart, K. (2004). Sticks and stones and shotguns at school: The ineffectiveness of constitutional antibullying legislation as a response to school violence. *Georgia Law Review, 39,* 1109–1154.

Kochenderfer-Ladd, B., & Pelletier, M. E. (2008). Teachers' views and beliefs about bullying: Influences on classroom management strategies and students' coping with peer victimization. *Journal of School Psychology, 46,* 431–453.

Limber, S. P., & Small, M. A. (2003). State laws and policies to address bullying in schools. *School Psychology Review, 32*(3), 445–455.

Miller, C. K. (2009, February 11). *Bullying: Understanding attitudes toward bullying and perceptions of school climate.* Retrieved from https://www.education.com/reference/article/student-attitudes-towards-bullying/

Rettner, R. (2010, August 26). *Bullies on bullying: Why we do it.* Retrieved from https://www.livescience.com/11163-bullies-bullying.html

Wight, S. (2008). Homeschooling can help prevent school bullying. In B. Rosenthal (Ed.), *Bullying* (pp. 49–54). Farmington Hill, MI: Greenhaven Press.

CHAPTER 7

It's a Mad, Mad, Mad World
Mean World Syndrome (Media Effects)

Perhaps the reason why students and (some) adults maintain the belief that bullying is inevitable and a part of the natural world order can be traced back to "mean world syndrome." MWS is an off-shoot of the cultivation theory posited by George Gerbner in the 1970s. Gerbner suggested that consumers of television and movies are influenced by the images and messages they receive. In other words, cultivation operates similarly to the "you are what you eat" adage repeated by parents to their children. The pervasiveness of mediated bullying may, in fact, feed the idea that bullying is a normal part of our reality.

> **Building a Bully-Free Building**
>
> This lesson helps students begin to think about what a school without name-calling and bullying might look and sound like.
> https://www.glsen.org/sites/default/files/Elementary%20Lesson-Building%20a%20Bully-free%20Building.pdf

Cultivation theory has been supported in numerous studies Which confirmed that media plays a role in the development of political ideologies (framing). Butler, Koopman, and Zimbardo (1995) and Feldman and Sigelman (1985), Mulligan and Habel (2011) sought to identify whether fictional films affect viewers' attitudes about the issue of the legality and morality of abortion. The treatment group viewed the 1999 film, *Cider House Rules,* a film that frames the abortion issue through the lens of a person whose pregnancy was the result of incest. The film's central theme presents a pro-choice message consistent with a political communication frame. In addition to the viewers' attitudes regarding abortion, the researchers also wanted to see the effect of the film on the issue of morality (defined as following one's conscience rather than following a code of conduct). One hundred and ninety-four undergraduates students enrolled in an introductory political science course at a Midwestern university participated in the study. 99 students were randomly assigned to a treatment group where they completed a questionnaire after watching the *Cider House Rules*. The control group completed the questionnaire only. Researchers found that that those who watched the film were more likely to agree with the moral message of the film as well as expressing a more pro-choice attitude for abortion in the context of the film. Contrary to their initial expectations, the film did not appear to change attitudes about the issue of abortion outside of the context of the film. This study suggests that fictional film can play a role in the development of students' attitudes about provocative subjects.

Mulligan and Habel (2012) extends previous research on testing the effects of feature films on the political attitudes and beliefs of viewers. In their previous study in 2011, they offer evidence that fictional media has an effect upon political attitudes. In this study, they examine whether the film *Wag the Dog* impacts viewers' trust in the American government. This study is informed by Butler, Koopman, and Zimbardo (1995) that tested whether the conspiracy theories surrounding President Kennedy's assassination in Oliver Stone's *JFK* affected viewers' political attitudes. Consistent with the literature on fictional media, Mulligan and Habel (2012) postulate that viewers are willing to suspend disbelief of fictional when the viewers/readers have perceptions of realism and connection to the film or book. They question whether that realism is influenced by the familiarity of the setting of the film. They postulate that fiction is less influential when the setting is "close to home" (p. 6). This question remains whether films watched in a classroom setting has a similar effect. Will viewers who watch a fictional film suspend belief because the film is shown for educational purposes? Does that boost its potential realism?

Mulligan and Habel (2012) offered course credit to 191 undergraduate students in an introductory course in U.S. politics at a medium Midwestern university. Participants were randomly assigned to a control and treatment group. Both groups were shown the same five slides giving matching details of the action of the film [the treatment group would also watch the film]. In the film, *Wag the Dog*, the president of the United States couples with a Hollywood producer to stage a fake war to cover up a scandal involving an illicit sexual affair just prior to his reelection bid. After being shown the five slides, participants answered two questions on the likelihood that the real president would stage a fake war and whether they believed that a fake war had actually been staged in the past. Results showed that those who deemed the film more realistic were more likely to be affected by the content—they were significantly more likely to believe that a fake war was possible and had already occurred. This study underscores the role of fictional narratives on affecting consumers' attitudes and beliefs and supports the need to understand film's potential impact upon their values and beliefs.

In an experimental field study, Butler et al. (1995) question the extent to which watching the controversial film *JFK* influenced audience emotions, beliefs, attitudes and behaviors. 107 adults who were entering (n=53) or exiting (n=54) a local movie theater were given self reporting paper-based surveys (55 males, 52 females). The surveys included demographic profiles, mood ratings (hopeful, angry, fearful, energized), intended political activities, beliefs in the likelihood of the film actions, general political beliefs regarding Americans' knowledge of government, and perceptions of the credulity of the conspiracies espoused in the film. As expected, the politically controversial film aroused feelings of anger and changed respondents' beliefs towards accepting the conspiracy theories. While post-viewing results indicated increased mood, beliefs, and judgments, the surveys indicate that these changes did not carry over into the general, real-life attitudes towards politics in general. On the measure related to intended behaviors, respondents reported a significant post-viewing intent to vote or make political contributions. One positive effect was that viewers suggested an increased intent to strengthen their commitment to become more informed about matters of government. "The implications of our findings that emotions, beliefs, and behavioral intentions can be significantly influenced by a movie such as *JFK* should strongly underscore concern that the media, even the cinema where fiction and fact may be unabashedly indistinguishable, is a powerful tool both for education and for misinformation" (p. 255).

In their study on the impact of watching a prime-time television docudrama on nuclear war, Feldman and Sigelman (1985) found that watching a television film had minimal effects on the attitudes of viewers. In November 1983, the ABC network aired a film titled "The Day After" which exemplifies life following a nuclear attack on America. According to the authors, the film caused a public uproar in print and television media. Their study sought to understand the effects of watching this film, particularly related to how it might shed new light on the political impact of prime-time television. The study took place in Lexington, KY. 496 respondents completed two rounds of phone interviews lasting 8–10 minutes each. The first wave of calls (random dialing) took place during the week prior to the airing of the film and the second wave was ten days after the airing. The measures included questions related to general attitudes towards military defense issues and towards the national government's treatment of the issues, beliefs regarding perceived knowledge about and likelihood of nuclear war, and their chances regarding survival after an attack. Consistent with other studies of this nature, measures regarding perceived realism were included (realism was found to have little bearing on results except for in the area dealing with military spending). The authors indicate that the tremendous media coverage of the film may have poisoned the participants as their findings indicate that much of the *total* impact of the film resulted more from the media attention than from viewing the film itself. While the article did not list the demographics of the participants, the researchers indicated that education seemed to be the most intervening variable; less educated viewers expressed more worry about nuclear war and about the defense spending strategies of then-President Ronald Reagan.

1 Mean World Syndrome and Bullying

In 2001, the American Academy of Pediatrics "recognized exposure to violence in media, including television, movies, music, and video games, as a significant risk that compromises the health of children and adolescents" (Kuntsche, Pickett, Overpeck, Craig, Boyce, & de Matos, 2006, p. 908).

Kuntsche (2004) established a link between students' feelings of a lack of safety in school and existence of bullying in school correlated to overexposure to violence in television viewing. "This study concluded that viewpoints learned from television might make the schoolyard appear to be a dangerous place, in most cases as a consequence of bullying and not physical aggression" (Kuntsche et al., 2006, p. 909). Consistent with these studies, Zimmerman, Glew, Christakis, and Katon (2005) saw a linked correlation between violent television exposure around age four and becoming a bully between ages six and eleven.

A new term "acquired violence immune deficiency syndrome" (Dyson, 2011) seeks to understand the "virus of violence" (Grossman, 1998) that seems to have infected youth and adolescent culture and contributes to the school shootings and fighting. Potter (2002) expects school violence to increase, arguing "Because the emerging generation of children already appears to be more accepting of violence and more prone to act aggressively and violently" (p. viii), although he suggests that media may not be the blame and makes for an easy scapegoat.

1.1 *Transportation Effects*

Transportation into a narrative world is described as the processes by which a reader or viewer is "transported" emotionally and cognitively into a fictional narrative text or film. Transportation is attributed to the manner whereby narratives can affect beliefs. It is also described as absorption and may be the mechanism which dictates viewers' enjoyment of a film or text. This transportation causes deeper connections with characters, make storylines believable, and is the conduit through which narratives shape beliefs and attitudes.

According to Green, Brock, and Kaufmann (2004), transportation is a "distinct mental process, an integrative melding of attention, imagery, and feelings" (p. 312). They indicate that film, more than literary texts, are particularly effective for transportation because viewers are more likely to respond to the visual imagery. This theoretical article provides an overview of the factors that may impact the relationship between transportation and enjoyment. These authors suggest that transportation is a "desired state" (p. 314) when consuming movies and is essential for enjoyment. Feature films are often able to pull people in through appeals to emotionality—this is particularly true of dramatic films. They indicate that there are numerous influences affecting enjoyment: how well-crafted and detailed the narrative; situational factors such as whether there are distractions in the theater, and plausibility of the action.

Many films that feature bullying behaviors fall into the comedy genre. While laughter and bullying are seemingly strange bedfellows, gelotophobia (the fear of being laughed at) (Ruch & Proyer, 2008) may be attributed to the abundance of images in comedy movies. Perhaps our "schadenfreude obsessed culture is to blame" (Franklin, 2015, p. 176). Schadenfreude can be defined as laughter at the expense of other's pain. A question worthy of further investigation is how much does exposure to comedic bullying contribute to bullying behaviors among youth and adolescents?

In his documentary video titled *The Mean World Syndrome* available from the Media Education Foundation, Gerbner questioned the use of comedic represenetations of violence. He concluded humor makes the pill easier to swallow. Humor is an excellent communication device because the pill is the pill of power: Who can get away with what against whom." By paying attention to the overall cultural story being promulgated by media depictions, violence—whether it's meant to be humorous or silly or not—is not simply the quantity of violence that now saturates the media landscape, but how it all adds up to tell a story—a story that reinforces and normalizes a certain view of the world. In this way, it is not simply the violent acts on their own, but the meaning of all this violence that has the greatest effect on those who are immersed in it.

Gerbner challenged the assumption that human beings were merely passive consumers of media and that media operated some immediate power over actions. Viewers have the ability *and* responsibility to behave appropriately despite what the media suggests. As an institution, Hollywood film has significant influence over American culture and the individual's understanding of the world. Critical theory explains the power of mass media to dictate the personal and societal: how film related to the broader historical context, how portrayals became representations, and how viewers actively or passively received the film's messages (Moss & Pavesich, 2011). It is concerned with how mainstream media (in this case, films) can be seen as a "reflector" of our national opinion; and, how the "culture industry" (Horkheimer & Adorno,

1972, p. 120) of instant gratification for viewers and arts-for-profit for directors and studio executives released easily reproducible, formulaic content. The studios are often at the mercy of a public that is satisfied with familiar themes, clearly identifiable characters, and expected conclusions. Early critical theorists did not necessarily focus on the topic of bullying as depicted in film, but they might certainly be interested in the study of the normative nature of contemporary film with regard to film's effects upon individuals' thinking and behavior (Garlick, 2011). Critical theory concerns itself with the notion that reality, like film, is constructed within a cultural context; and, the frequency of these images in mass-produced films then aid in the perpetuation of cultural norms and mores.

Lessem and Schieffer (2010) proffer four types of mechanisms that mirror the industry practice for repeated patterns of bullying in film in film: (1) promoting a dominant social identity while subordinating others; (2) a limited/limiting perspective rather than multiple models; (3) through manipulative communication, and; (4) by making subordinate groups invisible. A thorough examination of the film clips contained in this volume exemplifies these patterns. Victims tend to be targeted as sexual, religious, and racial minorities or as social outcasts, or for being the "new kid" or some other social outlier. The bullies themselves are depicted as a monolith—popular kids or athletes desiring to maintain social status at the "top of the food chain." A great example of this can be found in the film *A Girl Like Her*. This 2015 film is powerful in its depictions as it can be described as a "real life" model of the mean world we live in. The film's marketing strategy uses the tagline "Everybody's Dreamgirl. One Girl's Nightmare." The movie poster suggests that the film is "based on a million true stories" adding a pseudo-veracity to the scripted fictional tale. The film's website www.agirllikehermovie.com cites a quote from *People* magazine citing "although the film is a work of fiction, it's premise is an everyday reality for many kids." This marketing ploy thoroughly celebrates mean-world syndrome as it validates that bullying should be expected as a daily experience in our schools. Similarly, the website cites *Time* magazine, "*A Girl Like Her* shows what's really going on in American schools" (http://agirllikehermovie.com).

In the film, Jessica Burns (Lexi Ainsworth) endures unbearable amounts of harassment from her former best friend, Avery Keller (Hunter King). Jessica's friend, Brian (Jimmy Bennett) purchases secret spyware for Jessica to secretly record the daily bullying. It's perfect timing as their high school has been selected as a model high school and a film company is on campus to record daily life. Jessica's suicide attempt is foremost on the students' minds and becomes a focal point in the documentary footage [42:13–44:27].

Media literacy education in our schools may help students to become more critical regarding portrayals of violence and may inhibit feelings of helplessness to stop bullying behaviors promoted in movies.

References

Dyson, R. A. (2011). The mean world syndrome diminishes human security. *Journal of Human Security, 7*(1), 1–6.

Grossman, D. (1998). Trained to kill. *Christianity Today, 10*, 31–39.

Horkheimer, M., & Adorno, T. (1972). *Dialectic of enlightenment.* New York, NY: Herder & Herder.

Kuntsche, E., Pickett, W., Overpeck, M., Craig, W., Boyce, W., & de Matos, M. G. (2006). Television viewing and forms of bullying among adolescents from eight countries. *Journal of Adolescent Health, 39*(6), 908–915.

Moss, L., & Pavesich, V. (2011). Science, normativity and skill: Reviewing and renewing the anthropological basis of critical theory. *Philosophy and Social Criticism, 37*(2), 139–165.

Ruch, W., & Proyer, R. T. (2008). The fear of being laughed at: Individual and group differences in gelotophobia. *Humor, 21*(1), 47.

Zimmerman, F. J., Glew, G. M., Christakis, D. A., & Katon, W. (2005). Early cognitive stimulation, emotional support, and television watching as predictors of subsequent bullying among grade-school children. *Archives of Pediatrics & Adolescent Medicine, 159*(4), 384–388.

CHAPTER 8

Advise & Consent
Legal Policy and Bullying

Teachers and school administrators may find themselves living in a world of gray when it comes to dealing with bullying issues. The advances in technology and online communication have produced complex legal issues. Many teachers and school administrators are left wondering what they can legally do to address bullying, patricianly when it happens off school grounds. This chapter will explore historical legal cases that set a precedence on how schools can responds to complex situations in school.

The Supreme Court proclaimed the Internet a unique and wholly new medium (O'Neil, 2008), but laws have not caught up to this new medium. Hinduja and Patchin (2011) stated a "key issue facing educators with respect to cyberbullying prevention and response is the extent to which school officials have the right to restrict student expressions or to discipline for behavior or speech deemed inappropriate" (p. 72).

"Bullying may trigger legal responsibilities for schools under the civil rights laws enforced by the Office of Civil Rights (OCR) and the Department of Justice (DOJ) that prohibit discrimination and harassment based on race, color, national origin, sex, disability, and religion" (Duncan, 2010, p. 1). Title VI of the Civil Rights Act of 1964 prohibits discrimination on the basis of race, color, or national origin (U.S. Department of Justice, 2013). Title IX of the 1972 Education Amendments, prohibits discrimination on the basis of sex (U.S. Department of Labor, 2013). Section 504 of the Rehabilitation Act of 1973 (U.S. Dept. of Health and Human Services, 2006) as well as Title II of the Americans with Disability Act 1990 (Americans with Disabilities, 2010), prohibits discrimination on the basis of disability.

School leaders are faced with the challenge of addressing cyberbullying issues while not infringing on the rights of students. "The legal aspect of cyberbullying is critically important because school leaders need to know how courts judge their work in addressing cyberbullying" (Hvidston, Hvidston, Range, & Harbour, 2013, p. 2). Despite the complexities faced by school officials, "the U.S. Supreme Court has not yet specifically addressed cyberbullying in any of its decisions" (Hvidston et al., 2013, p. 3). However, there have been a number of court cases which address issues of harassment, 1st Amendment Rights, and the duty of school officials.

In the case of *Davis v. Monroe County Board of Education* (1999) the "U.S. Supreme Court ruled that under Title IX, schools and school districts may be liable for student-on-student harassment with deliberate indifference" (Willard & Alley, 2008, p. 200). Legally, deliberate indifference is when you have a reckless disregard for someone's actions (Davis v. Monroe County Board of Education, 1999). A school official may have knowledge of harassment taking place, but does not attempt to address the issue. By not addressing the issue the school official puts the well-being, health, and safety of the student at risk. In regards to the case of Davis v. Monroe County Board of Education, the court found that the school officials have a duty to intervene particularly when the harassment has a direct effect on a student's education (Davis v. Monroe County Board of Education, 1999).

The case of *Tinker v. Des Moines Independent Community School District* was argued in 1969, but is still widely cited today. Two students (a brother and sister) and their friend created a plan to wear black armbands to school to protest the Vietnam War. The school principal got word of the plan, and implemented a school policy that anyone wearing black armbands would be suspended. The three students decided to wear the armbands to school and were suspended. The students filed a suit in the U.S. District Court in Iowa. The court ruled in favor of the school district. The students appealed, and went to the U.S. Court of Appeals. The court of appeals ended in a tie, and later the case went to the U.S. Supreme Court. The U.S. Supreme Court ruled that the school would not prohibit symbolic or political speech unless the speech would results in a material and substantial disruption of normal school activities (Tinker v. Des Moines Independent Community School District, 1969). The Tinker Test has been applied to other cases. In addition, the language of substantial disruption of schools activities can be found in current education policies.

Although some cases still apply the Tinker Test, there have been situations where incidents occur that do not result in a disruption to the school environment. One example is the case of *Layshock v. Hermitage School District* in Pennsylvania. In this case, a high school student made an online parody of his high school principal. The principal found out about this, and suspended the student. The student was forced to finish high school at an alternative program. A federal judge ruled that the suspension was unconstitutional, and violated the students' 1st Amendment Rights. The court did not see where the online parody had a substantial disruption on the school environment (Layshock v. Hermitage School District, 2007). The Layshock case in an excellent example of how you can apply the Tinker Test, but it works in the favor of the student.

The 2007 case of *Morse v. Frederick* dealt with First Amendment Rights of students. The students at Juneau-Douglas High School, in Alaska, were allowed to leave class to watch the passing of the Olympic Torch. However, Joseph Frederick and his friends decided to stand on the sidewalk across the street from the school. At the exact moment the television cameras were around, Frederick and his friends held a banner which read Bong Hits 4 Jesus. During this time, the principal, Deborah Morse, went across the street and took the banner away. Frederick was suspended on the grounds of violating the school district's anti-drug policy.

In 2002 Frederick filed a lawsuit against the principal and the school board claiming his right to free speech had been violated. The U.S. District Court in Alaska rule that Morse and the school board did not violate Frederick's First Amendment rights. The court held that the principal had reason to interpret the banner as violating the school's policy on drug use. Frederick appealed and the case was taken to the Ninth Circuit Court. The Ninth Circuit Court reversed the decision stating that the banner was not sponsored or endorsed by the school, it did not occur at an official school activity, and the banner was not made as part of the curriculum, for example an art class (Morse v. Frederick, 2007).

The relevant cases illustrate that school officials are able to intervene if a situation leads to a substantial disruption of the school environment. The cases also show that school officials have a duty and responsibility to protect vulnerable students such as lesbian, gay, bisexual and transgendered (LGBT) students. School administrators would not be violating a student's freedom of expression rights, if that expression or speech were an attack or threat to other students. In addition, school officials are responsible for the welfare of students.

Although there are many court cases that give support to teachers and school administrators to address behavior, there is still much work to be done regarding addressing bullying in laws. In 1999 Georgia became the first state to pass an anti-bullying law (BullyPolice, 2017). States update laws and various groups have monitored these laws. One in particular is The Bully Police USA. According to their website The Bully Police USA is a watchdog organization, which advocates for bullied children and reporting on state anti-bullying laws (BullyPolice, 2017a). The Bully Police not only grades each state based on their state laws on a scale from A-F, but provides a checklist on what states should include in their anti-bullying policy (High, 2017). We strongly encourage any school teacher, administrator, parent or concerned citizen to use these resources and check with your own state about its current anti-bullying laws.

What does an anti-bullying law need? According to The Bullying Police an anti-bullying state law should include the following:

- The word "bullying" must be used in the text of the bill
- The law must clearly be an anti-bullying law and not a school safety law
- The law should clearly define both bullying and harassment
- There should be recommendations about how to make policy and what needs to be in a model policy
- A comprehensive law must include educational specialists at each level: school district, schools, parents, and the superintendent's office
- Must mandate anti-bullying programs and not suggest them
- Include specific dates that the policy is due
  - When schools should have their policies in place
- Must include protection against reprisal, retaliation or false accusations
- Protect school teachers and administrators who comply with policies from lawsuits
- Focus on the victim and helping to arrange counseling services
- Accountability in place for school and school districts who do not comply with the anti-bullying law
- Must have a clause addressing cyberbullying/electronic harassment (BullyPolice, 2017e).

As mentioned earlier, the BullyPolice watchdog group grades each state based on the adherence to this checklist. The good news is that as of March 2015 all states have passed some form of anti-bullying law. Currently, there are no states with a grade of a D or F. We will explore some of the states that are doing exceptionally well, and some that could use improvement. Please be sure to go to the BullyPolice website to gain more in-depth information about all of the anti-bullying state laws.

> **Featured Website**
> Bully Police
> www.bullypolice.org
> A Watch-dog Organization—
> Advocating for Bullied Children &
> Reporting on State Anti Bullying
> Laws

Being named the Best Anti-Bullying Law written to date is no easy task, but Florida has earned the honor (BullyPolice, 2017b). In 2008 Florida passed H.B. 669—School Safety or commonly referred to as Jeffrey Johnston Stand Up for All Students Act (BullyPolice, 2017b). Jeffrey Johnston was a young student in Florida who committed suicide at 15 years old after countless incidents of bullying at school, and online (Chang, Owen, & Brady, 2008). H.B. 669 prohibits the bullying or harassment of any student or school employee. The bill has a clause regarding procedures for reporting incidents to parents (BullyPolice, 2017b). The bill requires that all victims be able to seek counseling. Across the board the Florida bill checks off major components. The bill includes both cyberbullying and online harassment. There are both school sanctions as well as criminal sanctions for cyberbullying (Cyberbullying Research Center, 2017). Each school is required to have a policy against bullying. The bill includes off-campus incidents which impact the school environment (Cyberbullying Research Center, 2017).

In 2001 Louisiana passed H.B. 364, Act 230. The state law earned an average grade of C (BullyPolice, 2017c). H.B. 364 does make reference to cyberbullying and off-campus behavior. The law protects any student or school employee who reports any incidents of bullying, harassment and intimidation. Under this law, each school would be required to adopt a zero tolerance policy regarding fighting in school (BullyPolice, 2017c). If a student is expelled for fighting the law requires the student(s) to attend and pay for conflict resolution classes. The parents of the expelled student would also be required to attend the class (BullyPolice, 2017c).

Contest
(Contest LLC, 2013)
8:26–10:26

Minnesota earns a grade of C- for their state law (BullyPolice, 2017d). In 2007 Minnesota passed their anti-bullying law H.F. No. 504. Despite its passage, the bill falls short in key areas. The law says that each school should have an anti-bullying policy; it does not give specific details on regarding dates for the policy to be in effect (BullyPolice, 2017d). In addition, the Minnesota law does not provide any sort of accountability plan. While the bill clearly defines cyberbullying and online harassment, it does not set any criminal sanction for anyone found in violation of cyberbullying or electronic harassment (Cyberbullying Research Center, 2017).

Nevada passed State Law, A.B. 459 in 2011. The law earned a grade of B+ (BullyPolice, 2017e). The law requires the Department of Education for the state to create an educational program addressing and prohibiting harassment, intimidation and discrimination in schools. Each school district is required to use the policy developed by the Nevada Department of Education. The schools must offer educational training for their school employees (BullyPolice, 2017e). While the law required educational training, it does fall short in certain areas. The Nevada law includes criminal sanctions for cyberbullying or electronic harassment but does not include any school sanctions for cyberbullying (Cyberbullying Research Center, 2017). The law does not mention any sanctions for behavior that occurs off campus that disrupts the school environment (Cyberbullying Research Center, 2017).

The BullyPolice group gives New Jersey an A++. In 2002 New Jersey's Assembly Education Committee passed (AB) 1874 (BullyPolice, 2017f). The bill would require all school employees, students or volunteers to report any incidents of bullying, intimation and harassment. Schools districts must adopt a policy on anti-bullying and provide a copy to all county schools and superintendent (Bullypolice, 2017f). The schools work with the Commissioner of Education in order to develop their policy (Bullypolice, 2017f). New Jersey is one of few states which checks yes on all major components of an anti-bullying policy. The law includes cyberbullying and online harassment. It includes details on criminal sanction for violations of cyberbullying or electronic harassment. The school must provide a detailed policy on how to address bullying issues (Bullypolice, 2017f). The New Jersey law states that action can be taken for off-campus behavior that disrupts the school environment. Finally, schools can provide sanctions for cyberbullying (Cyberbullying Research Center, 2017). New Jersey provides a detailed law that clearly defines bullying and includes sanctions for cyberbullying. The BullyPolice says that a law does not get a grade of A++ unless there is attention placed on the victim receiving free counseling. An A++ law must have a clause relating specifically to cyberbullying (High, 2017). It looks like New Jersey sets up standards with their comprehensive state law.

Keeping up to date with state laws regarding bullying can be a challenge. Gone are the days where the bullying stopped when the school bell rang at 3:00pm. Today, students are faced with technology that allows for comments, videos, and text messages to be sent 24 hours a day. Despite the constant flow of data, states are continuing to work, to create laws that help protect students and school administrators. All laws have not caught up to the ever changing technologies. Despite the work that needs to happen, we know that the language used in the law, and creating a detailed policy is a critical step in the right direction. The goal is to remember to keep the best interest of the victim in mind, and ensure they get the proper resources.

Everyone from students, parents, teachers, and community leaders can play a role to help address the ever growing issue on bullying in school and online. Parents can play an active role by talking with their children about online activity. Parents should also be encouraged to go to the schools and make contact with the principal and as their child's teacher. The key to have communication and make sure everyone know about the school policy on bullying and the protocol for reporting incidents. Everyone can have an impact by starting at the local level. Go to parent-teacher conferences and inquire about the school's policy on bullying. Contact your local state representative and ask about where bullying is on their agenda. The work of getting comprehensive anti-bullying laws passed is not easy, but with hard work and getting multiple players involved can help make for positive change. For anyone who wants more information on bullying laws or reading material, below is a list of helpful resources to check out.

Helpful Resources

Bullycide in America: Moms Speak out About Bullying/Suicide by Brenda High (2012)

This is not a book about blame or guilt, although it may certainly spark that kind of discussion. This is not a book about getting even or setting the record straight, although it may do that as well. And, this is not a book for clinicians, although it will offer some scientific data and educational resources. This is a book of real stories about real kids. Kids who took their own lives because they thought it was their only way out of a hopeless situation.

Bullying Prevention Podcast

This podcast discusses the crucial role educators play in bullying prevention.

Cyberbullying Research Center (https://cyberbullying.org/)

This website serves as a clearinghouse of information concerning the ways adolescents use and misuse technology. It is intended to be a resource for parents, educators, law enforcement officers, counselors, and others who work with youth (as well as for youth themselves). Here you will find facts, figures, and detailed stories from those who have been directly impacted by online aggression.

Megan Meier Foundation (https://www.meganmeierfoundation.org/)

To Support and Inspire Actions to End Bullying, Cyberbullying, and Suicide. The foundation provides resources for parents, teachers, and students through workshops and presentations.

Not in Our School (https://www.niot.org/nios/quickstart)

The Not In Our School (NIOS) Quick Start Guide will help you mobilize students to be "upstanders" who take action to stand up for another and create a climate that reflects the values of safety, respect, and inclusion.

StopBullying (https://www.stopbullying.gov/)

StopBullying.gov coordinates closely with the Federal Partners in Bullying Prevention Steering Committee, an interagency effort led by the Department of Education that works to coordinate policy, research, and communications on bullying topics.

Disclaimer

Neither of the authors are lawyers or legal professionals. This chapter does not constitute legal advice. Please refer to your school's legal counsel and administration for advice.

References

BullyPolice. (2017a). *Homepage.* Retrieved from http://www.bullypolice.org/
BullyPolice. (2017b). *Florida.* Retrieved from http://www.bullypolice.org/fl_law.html
BullyPolice. (2017c). *Louisiana.* Retrieved from http://www.bullypolice.org/la_law.html
BullyPolice. (2017d). *Minnesota.* Retrieved from http://www.bullypolice.org/mn_law.html
BullyPolice. (2017e). *Nevada.* Retrieved from http://www.bullypolice.org/nv_law.html
BullyPolice. (2017f). *New Jersey.* Retrieved from http://www.bullypolice.org/nj_law.html
Chang, J., Owen, L., & Brady, J. (2008, May 2). *Mom's campaign for Florida anti-bullying law pays finally off.* Retrieved from http://abcnews.go.com/GMA/story?id=4774894
Cyberbullying Research Center. (2017). *Bullying laws across America.* Retrieved from https://cyberbullying.org/bullying-laws
Davis v. Monroe County Board of Education. (1999). 120 F.3d 1390.
Duncan, A. (2010). *Dear colleagues letter.* Retrieved from http://www2.ed.gov/policy/gen/guid/secletter/101215.html
High, B. (2017). *Making the grade: How States are "graded" on their anti-bullying laws.* Retrieved from http://www.bullypolice.org/grade.html
Hinduja, S., & Patchin, J. W. (2011). Cyberbullying: A review of legal issues facing educators. *Preventing School Failure: Alternative Education for Children and Youth, 55*(2), 71–78. doi:10.1080/1045988X.2011.539433
Layshock v. Hermitage School District. (2007). 496 F. Supp. 2d 587, 600–02.
Morse v. Frederick. (2007). 551 U.S. 393, 127 S. Ct. 2618.
O'Neil, R. M. (2008). It's not easy to stand up to cyberbullies, but we must. *The Chronicle of Higher Education: Commentary, 54*(44), A23–A28.
Tinker v. Des Moines Independent Community School District. (1969). 393 U.S. 503.
U.S. Department of Justice. (2013). *Overview of title vi of the civil rights acts of 1964.* Retrieved from http://www.justice.gov/crt/about/cor/coord/titlevi.php

CHAPTER 9

Lean on Me
The Role of the Teacher as Intervener

In schools across the country, administrators have relied on paid "experts" to give a canned anti-bullying presentation to students at a special program or assembly. This *ad hoc* approach does little to change the culture within classrooms and hallways (Bickmore, 2011). Lane (1989) argues that schools have de-prioritized anti-bullying giving deference to truancy and policy-making. As long as curbing bullying is an afterthought, the problem will persist. This text supports the idea that administrations would do well to empower their teachers to be the front line "first responders" when it comes to the everyday interventions that can facilitate culture change.

> **Anti-Bullying Week: Primary School Pack**
> Empower students to help celebrate what makes them, and others, unique
> https://www.anti-bullyingalliance.org.uk/sites/default/files/field/attachment/Primary_School_Pack%20-%20FINAL.pdf

Few would debate the important role teachers play for dealing with bullying behaviors in the classroom and school building. They often are called upon to report bullying activities "when they see it," but what we are suggesting is their necessity in creating an atmosphere where bullying is discouraged—not by a special once-per-year, special observance, but by making regular curricular interventions. This chapter provides lessons and activities teachers can use with their students in a classroom setting.

Teachers already model appropriate behavior and step in when bullying happens in plain sight, but what if they were to create opportunities for dialogue and for students to "learn" how to speak up and stand up when they see bullying around them? Anti-bullying "education" and campaigns are a staple in elementary schools, but fizzle out of importance and rotation in the middle and high schools—the presumption being that students "get it" in elementary school and should know how to be a good citizen when they get older. Imagine if that was our approach to mathematics education? Taking a more active approach to anti-bullying education has the potential to signal to kids that the school/classroom is a safe space and bullying and targeting others is unacceptable (Veenstra, Lindenberg, Huitsing, Sainio, & Salmivalli, 2014).

Furthermore, regular interventions bolster students' abilities to call out negative behaviors and to name bullying. The Department of Homeland Security uses the campaign slogan "If you see something, say something" as a mechanism in their anti-terror work. In essence, this slogan deputizes each traveler to act when something is out of sorts (Reeves, 2012). Perhaps regular attention by teachers can affect the school climate create in the same way.

This is particularly true when underscoring the role of movies and popular media. Our students may need help to "see" bullying in real life when they are bombarded by the negative images in film and television—much of which is shrouded in comedic themes. When we are programmed to laugh at bullying in entertainment media, our ability to take responsibility to act may be diminished. In fact, we may be inclined to laugh and/or participate.

Educators using film to educate may need to reprogram students to interpret what they see as negative and harmful and to orient themselves as actors. In the following activity, students view a movie clip and identify the various roles individuals in the scene play.

Suggested Activity

Show students a film clip and have them answer the following questions:
- Who is the victim?
- Who is the bully?
- What type of bullying was it?
- What harm did the bully do?
- Why did the bully do what they did?
- If you were the victim, what would you do?

The following clips can be useful with this exercise:
2:37 18:00–19:15
Anger Management 0:57–2:42
Bridge to Terabithia 41:13–42:50
A Christmas Story 21:50–23:59
Diary of a Wimpy Kid 1:20:40–1:24:32

This simple exercise enables students to interpret visual stimuli to be able to identify problematic behavior.

What makes the teacher the ideal person to do this important work is the relationship that is forged in the classroom. To admit you've been the victim of bullying or you've witnessed bullying is very difficult. Students need trusted individuals to call on. As a regular point of connection, the teacher can be a great resource for students.

Teachers can help students develop their lexicons to talk about bullying. May students may not have the vocabulary to correctly name or identify their associated feelings. Regular classroom talk can empower students to have the confidence and assertiveness to speak up even if it is uncomfortable to do so (Stables, 2009). The classroom also offers students an opportunity to practice anti-bullying skills in a safe, supportive environment.

Teachers can help create a "bullying prevention plan" for their classroom similar to the normative posters used to implement classroom behavior guidelines. This plan can identify what students should do if they witness a bullying event to include where and to whom they should report.

In these regular classroom interventions, teachers can spur students' creativity to develop exercises and activities that can be used as simulations. According to the Room 241 website sponsored by the Concordia University-Portland, theater students in a Michigan high school developed a dramatic play on the theme of bullying and its aftermath (https://education.cu-portland.edu/blog/leaders-link/a-teachers-role-in-bullying-prevention/). A similar project was featured in the 2002 film *Bang, Bang, You're Dead* where troubled student, Trevor Adams (Ben Foster), participated in a performance where a bullied student brings a gun to school in a revenge plot.

The teacher is largely responsible for fostering an atmosphere of support for students. This is one of those "other duties as assigned" features of most faculty contracts. This atmosphere is designed to welcome all students regardless of identity—race, religion, sexual orientation, creed, etc. Signage in classrooms can serve in this area also to send a message to students of the protected space and the teacher as a trusted individual (Loverro, Majsterek, & Shorr, 2012).

Bullying is often "supported" in student culture unwittingly because of our society's inherent support of social dominance hierarchies. Regular classroom dialogue can expose the mythologies used to foster imbalanced and harmful attitudes. The development of social hierarchies "works" because individuals and groups operate under certain societal, shared ideologies. These myths shape public and personal consciousness about subordinate or superordinate groups and are traditionally maintained in values, beliefs, stereotypes, and cultural norms. Social dominance theory highlights two types of myths in operation in group-based inequity: hierarchy enhancing and hierarchy attenuating myths.

The enhancing myths offer rationalization of beliefs that support oppression and inequality such as racism and sexism. The general argument is that inequality is fair and a "natural" dimension of society. These ideologies sustain dominance at the personal, interpersonal, and group levels. Not only do majority-identified persons gain benefit from these myths, those in subordinate groups who share these ideals collaborate with those in majority groups to maintain oppression and inequality.

In contrast, hierarchy-attenuating myths offer support for equality and preference for more universal and human rights. Educational systems like universities tend to be attenuating institutions (Sidanius, Sinclair, & Pratto, 2006). Attenuating myths are in stark opposition to the beliefs consistent with hierarchy enhancing myths. Social dominance theory assumes that members of predominant groups will exhibit great support for enhancing mythologies more than those in targeted groups who give more credence to attenuating myths. Sidanius and Pratto (1999) established, however, that regardless of position, there is often more consensus for legitimizing myths across superordinate and subordinate groups. Again, this shared consensus is what produces and maintains hierarchical supports.

Legitimizing myths play a great deal in the development and support of individual discriminatory behaviors. Non-target groups often provide benefits to others within similar social strata. For instance, with regard to employment, super-ordinates have the ability to offer jobs to others within their affinity group while the poor and disenfranchised remain unemployed. These individual acts when aggregated over time provide a basis for inequality on a grand scale that is biased against those in target groups. The allocation of resources and power then falls to those in dominant positions or groups thereby giving them a more positive social value. This is not to say that all individuals in higher social or cultural classes believe and/or act in concert with hierarchy enhancing mythology, nor does this mean their attitudes are predetermined. The difference is most often contextual rather than randomly assigned; this has more to do with a person's social dominance orientation towards hierarchal group status preference.

Ramasubramanian (2010) examines the role of television portrayals as endorsing hierarchy enhancing or hierarchy attenuating legitimizing myths, specifically whether the stereotypes of Latinos and Blacks as lazy and prone to criminal behavior. Ramasubramanian (2010) examines how televised portrayals of African Americans and Latinos affect White viewers—particularly how these characterizations influence real-life attitudes and beliefs and whether these changes in attitude affect viewers' support for race-targeted policies, such as affirmative action. 323 undergraduates enrolled in a communications course completed a series of test measures about their perceptions of racial groups, their belief in stereotypes, attitudes of prejudice, and support for affirmative action programs.

To examine the perceived stereotypes of racial groups on television, participants were asked to reflect on their level of agreement with the common images depicted. Regarding depictions of minorities, two themes emerged: (1) perceived criminality and (2) laziness. They also completed a measure to examine their endorsement of real life stereotypes. The same themes of lazy criminals emerged. Regarding their own prejudicial feelings, respondents indicated their agreement with generalized statements about minority groups; racial prejudice, then, was measured regarding sentiments of ingroup superiority. In general, prejudicial feelings and towards minorities correlated with acceptance of televised minority characterizations as authentic. There was a lack of support for affirmative action programs regardless of priming for specific outgroups. What role does television (or film) characterization or themes play in hierarchy enhancing or attenuating ideology? Ramasubramanian (2010) argues that the "findings from this study strengthen the existing attitudinal literature that suggests that emotions are a greater predictor of behavioral intentions than are beliefs" (p. 116).

While the idea of social hierarchies benefit those in superior positions or groups, it is important to understand that there appears to be collusion between dominants and subordinate individuals and groups in the establishment and continuation of dominance. This "behavioral asymmetry" (Pratto et al., 2006) preferences dominant groups, at times, with the approval of the subordinate groups. There are three primary types of asymmetry: asymmetrical in-group bias, self-debilitation, and ideological asymmetry.

Asymmetrical in-group bias occurs when dominants display more in-group favoritism. This asymmetry is encouraged by people's affirmation of the legitimizing myths. If a social system is considered legitimate, dominant groups tend to display a higher degree of favor to like kind members than to subordinates. Sidanius and Pratto (1999) studied American adults' beliefs in the egalitarian nature of American society. Whites (dominants) showed higher levels of ethnic preference than those in targeted racial minority groups. In contrast, when respondents were primed with the value of American being unjust and unequal, members of minority groups exhibited higher levels of ethnic favoritism. When members of subordinate groups develop behaviors that can be deemed self-destructive, they contribute to their own self-debilitation.

The pervasiveness of attitudes in support of social hierarchies and the consistency of the legitimizing myths prevail, even in the arbitrary set system dimensions such as race and ethnicity, nationality, and religion. These topics are the most consistent in the literature about social dominance orientation. Yet, similarly, socioeconomic class and sexual orientation are culturally contextual in the development of rules and the manifestations of values—the standards of desirability and goodness. The following sections outline pertinent literature on the intersections of SDO and sexual orientation and socioeconomic class.

One such area that needs regular intervention is in the subject of Islamophobia that has been on the rise since September 11th 2001. National conversations, even from the President of the United States, identify Muslims as terrorists. The following media resources expose the mythologies potentially operating in your classroom.

This 9 minute video is excerpted from the ABC television reality show *What Would You Do?* (https://www.youtube.com/watch?v=6i_8ZWBE-5U). The clip reveals people's reactions to two students mistreating a Muslim student. View this 9-minute video. Showing this video on its own has the potential to spark dialogue about how to respond and the responsibility of bystanders, but is also raises critical awareness of issues faced my Muslim students that your "regular" students may not readily recognize. Incorporating this YouTube clip into a character education lesson compounds student learning.

American Bully
(MGM, 2003)
31:28–33:26
41:15–43:40
44:56–48:25

The 2003 film *American Bully* can support an educational intervention on discrimination towards Muslim students. In the film, a middle-Eastern teenage boy who is affected by 9/11, terrorism, and the war in Iraq becomes involved in an isolated high school altercation that escalates into a hate crime that shocks the entire nation. (CAUTION: This film is violent and is riddled with coarse language.)

Teachers may feel inhibited by the requirement to focus solely on subject matter and

Recognizing Discrimination

People sometimes look the other way when they see an act of discrimination because they do not know how to stop it. This lesson provides students with real-world examples to help them identify peaceful ways to respond.
https://www.tolerance.org/classroom-resources/tolerance-lessons/recognizing-discrimination

content. This type of teaching requires intentionality to find the connection to their content area. This also requires administrator buy-in and support. Those teaching language arts and social studies should more easily be able to integrate character education lessons into their curricula [*Lord of the Flies* (Golding, 1954) is a literary masterpiece centered around bullying] while those in the hard sciences, for instance, may need to get more creative to draw the connection. It's not impossible. The National Academies of Science, Engineering, and Medicine produced a resource called *Preventing Bullying Through Science, Policy, and Practice* (2016) where they integrate science, policy, and anti-bullying education. They review the "science" behind peer victimization, bullying behavior, and its consequences.

Special Note: It is important to remember the potential consequences when debating whether or not to include anti-bullying education into the curriculum – CHILDREN ARE DYING. That alone should be enough reason to include educational intervention.

Recommended Resource

Bullied | A Student, a School and a Case That Made History
Bullied is a documentary film available from the Southern Poverty Law Center's *Teaching Tolerance* arm that chronicles one student's ordeal at the hands of anti-gay bullies and offers an inspiring message of hope to those fighting harassment today.
  Available FREE to teachers from www.tolerance.org

Teachers need to regularly strive to foster an atmosphere of support when it comes to curbing bullying behavior. It's not just about "catching" the bullies, but also provoking goodness and kindness as essential to being a good citizen. The signs of bullying are sometimes difficult for teachers to catch—someone "accidentally" tripping someone in the hall, someone whispering cruel comments to belittle and embarrass another student. Promoting citizenship in a way that is not "hokey" or "corny" to students can go a long way in building our schools as effective democracies (Biesta & Lawy, 2006).

These interventions need not be held on a "special day," but need to be normed into the regular activities. Teachers need to be flexible and able to shift their content in the moment. A great example occurs in the 2007 film *Freedom Writers*. Mrs. Erin Gruwell (played by Hilary Swank) is a first time teacher at an impoverished school in the inner city. On this particular day [27:22–37:15], as Mrs. Gruwell is teaching a grammar lesson, a Latino student named Tito passes a racist caricature of a Black student named Jamal. When Mrs. Gruwell intercepts the handwritten drawing, she becomes incensed and explains how drawings like these led to the Jewish Holocaust. Many of the students in her class are members of rival gangs or territotial sects; Mrs. Gruwell belittles their group rivalry implying that the Nazis were "The most famous gang of all." She explains the Nazi regime's rise to power through violence and propaganda such as the drawing–"They just wiped out everybody else." She continues to describe how the caricatures of Blacks and Jews were used to justify violence against these groups; how scientific evidence was used to prove "Jews and Blacks were the lowest form of the human species. Jews and Blacks were just like animals; and because they were animals, it didn't really matter if they lived or died." Though a scripted scene, Mrs. Gruwell's immediate action opened a stream of dialogue where the students talked about their perceptions of race and racism and living in their home communities.

> **Teaching Strategy**
> **Barometers**
>
> The barometer teaching strategy helps students share their opinions by lining up along a continuum to represent their point of view. It is especially useful when trying to discuss an issue about which students have a wide range of opinions. Engaging in a barometer activity can be an effective pre-writing exercise before an essay assignment because it gets many arguments out on the table. For more information, visit https://www.facinghistory.org/for-educators/educator-resources/teaching-strategies/barometer-taking-stand-contro

References

Bickmore, K. (2011). Policies and programming for safer schools: Are "anti-bullying" approaches impeding education for peacebuilding? *Educational Policy, 25*(4), 648–687.

Biesta, G., & Lawy, R. (2006). From teaching citizenship to learning democracy: Overcoming individualism in research, policy and practice. *Cambridge Journal of Education, 36*(1), 63–79.

Lane, D. A. (1989). Bullying in school: The need for an integrated approach. *School Psychology International, 10*(3), 211–215.

Loverro, I. J., Majsterek, D. J., & Shorr, D. N. (2012). Signage as a classroom prompt: An evidence-based practice? In J. E. Aitken, J. P. Fairley, & J. K. Carlson (Eds.), *Communication technology for students in special education and gifted programs* (pp. 196–205). Hershey, PA: IGI Global.

National Academies of Sciences, Engineering, and Medicine. (2016). *Preventing bullying through science, policy, and practice*. Washington, DC: National Academies Press.

Ramasubramanian, S. (2010). Television viewing, racial attitudes, and policy preferences: Exploring the role of social identity and intergroup emotions in influencing support for affirmative action. *Communication Monographs, 77*(1), 102–120.

Reeves, J. (2012). If you see something, say something: Lateral surveillance and the uses of responsibility. *Surveillance & Society, 10*(3–4), 235–248.

Sidanius, J., Sinclair, S., & Pratto, F. (2006). Social dominance orientation, gender, and increasing educational exposure1. *Journal of Applied Social Psychology, 36*(7), 1640–1653.

Stables, A. (2009). Learning, identity and classroom dialogue. *The Journal of Educational Enquiry, 4*(1), 1–18.

Veenstra, R., Lindenberg, S., Huitsing, G., Sainio, M., & Salmivalli, C. (2014). The role of teachers in bullying: The relation between antibullying attitudes, efficacy, and efforts to reduce bullying. *Journal of Educational Psychology, 106*(4), 1135–1143.

CHAPTER 10

The Big Short
Film Clips for Instructional Use

The lessons in this book are designed to supplement your instruction on bullying-related issues. For each of the definitions listed earlier, you will find a movie clip that illustrates the concept you are teaching. Each clip lasts no longer than ten minutes. This volume uses clips from both mainstream blockbuster films and little-known independent gems. Many are available in your local library, on streaming sites such as Netflix, or in your school library. Consult your school's resource librarians for more assistance in obtaining films.

Perhaps the greatest single obstacle confronting teachers who want to use film during instruction is the schedule. Most teachers have less than an hour of classroom time (40–50 minutes on average), which doesn't give enough time to adequately review even a short film and have critical discussion. To use feature films, teachers must divide the film into three or four class periods. Understanding this challenge, this book has identified meaningful clips to watch that get at the heart of issues of difference.

Each illustration gives a brief statement on the content rating of the movie. Most of the descriptions are written in a way that assumes that the movie clip will not be shown—providing necessary plot summary and describing the crucial scene concretely—but does include elapsed times so the instructor can locate the scene easily if the film is actually used (*highly recommended*).

Please remember that these clips are designed to complement your instruction about the issues. Teaching these concepts is often controversial and, as stated earlier, students do not often possess the awareness, knowledge, and skills to be successful in these types of discussions. To effectively harness the power of these visual images, the teacher must prepare the students for what they might see and what they should be on the lookout for. This preparation should include providing information that is necessary for comprehension, including ensuring that students understand key terminology. Providing students with an overall context of the film is important, as well as helping them to understand how a particular clip fits into the film's action and story line.

THE BIG SHORT 61

> **IMPORTANT NOTE**
>
> *As the instructor, you must decide which clips are most suitable for your audience. You are responsible for ensuring that the content is developmentally and age-appropriate for your students, and that you have appropriate permissions to use film in your classroom. You are encouraged to screen the clips before using them in class.*

Please note that the running times are approximated and may vary depending upon the format of the recording. You have been provided enough detail in the scene descriptions that will help you locate the scene in any format. This method will help you find the scene quickly, even if you are unfamiliar with the film.

A Note about Using Copyrighted Materials

The Copyright Act allows for showing copyrighted film scenes during the course of regular classroom instruction. A teacher may not charge a fee for viewing the scenes and only students in the course are permitted to view (no public viewing). You must use a legal copy of the film that has either been rented or purchased. This instructional use provision within the copyright code does cover "home use" (see the FBI warning at the beginning of the video) rented videos for use in the classroom. You should consult the audiovisual staff or instructional media team at your institution for clarity on school policies for media use.

Here is a sample of the video clips included in this volume:

Title of Film	*Definition(s)*
Benchwarmers, The	**PHYSICAL/BYSTANDER**

Plot Summary

Three grown men with a childhood chip on their shoulders decide to take on all little league challengers in three-man baseball. They become the champions for all wannabes and social outcasts.

Scene Description

Three socially inept young children are playing baseball in the local park when members of the organized little league team try to force them off the diamond. One of the young kids argues that the team's practice does not start until

4:30; the team leader states "We want to have a practice before the practice." A girl who was with the original group suggests they all play together when an older boy retorts "No, because you suck. Why don't you go home and build your science projects." The oldest boy pushes the other boy down, and while another team member holds him, the oldest nearly sits on the boy's face and gives him some "beef stew" (he farted just above his nose). The young boy is rescued when an adult named Gus (played by Ron Schneider) chases the older boys away. In tears, the young boy tells Gus, "It actually didn't taste as bad as you'd think" and runs away. Gus ponders, "Why do kids have to be so fricking cruel?"

Film Citation

The Benchwarmers (Revolution Studios, 2006), written by Allen Covert & Nick Swardson and directed by Dennis Dugan
Elapsed Time: This scene begins at 0:50 and ends at 4:04
Rating: Rated PG-13 for crude and suggestive humor, and for language

Film Clips

2:37 HARASSMENT/BIAS

At 2:37, a student committed suicide in the school bathroom. The day is played out in the lives of six students as the story is told.

Luke is greeted in the school hallway by his friends. He asks what transpired at the party they attended after he left. Luke explains, "I was fuckin' gone, man." His friend agreed, "You were fucked." Luke tells the story how while he was in the bathroom, Ben tapped him on the shoulder. Luke turned around and "just piss[ed] all over this guy." "You fucking pissed all over him? What did Ben do?" Luke returns, "What could he do man? He was covered in piss." Just then, the boys sight Sean who is kneeling at his locker. The three circle around him and begin to taunt. "Hey Seany! How's it going, buddy? You'd get fucking shit on your dick?" They all laugh while the ribbing continues, "Hey, Sean, do you like taking it or giving it, huh?" They mimic sexual noises and acts. One of the boys adds, "Hey, come on, give us a kiss." Sean yells, "Get the fuck off me!" Luke questions, "We're not good enough for you, Seany?" Sean stares at each of them. As he walks off, he declares, "You're fucking pathetic." "One of the boys defends, "You fucking cock jockey!" The scene ends as Melody walks in and kisses her boyfriend.

2:37 (Kojo Pictures, 2006), written and directed by Murali K. Thalluri
Elapsed Time: This scene begins at 18:00 and ends at 19:15
Rating: Not rated

17 Again   PHYSICAL
Mike O'Donnell (Matt Leblanc) is on the verge of a mid-life crisis. Despite his marriage, family, and business success, he longs for happier days like his high school popularity. Magically, he is transported to the times he desires.

Teenager Mike O'Donnell (Zac Efron) is preparing to use the urinal when a voice from the stall pleads for help. When he peers over the stall, he sees his friend, Alex (Sterling Knight), wrapped in duct tape. Alex admits it was the basketball team who taped him. He says he'd offer to shake Mike's hand, "but it's taped to my ass." Mike offers to rip off the tape like a Band-Aid. The scene ends as Alex winces in pain.

17 Again (New Line, 2009), written by Jason Filardi and directed by Burr Steers
Elapsed Time: This scene begins at 35:03 and ends at 35:58
Rating: Rated PG-13 for language, some sexual material and teen partying

17 Again   REVENGE
Mike O'Donnell (Matt Leblanc) is on the verge of a mid-life crisis. Despite his marriage, family, and business success, he longs for happier days like his high school popularity. Magically, he is transported to the times he desires.

Alex (Sterling Knight) and Mike (Zac Efron) are in the cafeteria. Alex watches Stan (Hunter Parrish) and his basketball cronies enter the cafeteria. Alex admits, "I hate that guy." Mike gets Alex to admit that Stan is the one who taped him to the toilet in an earlier scene. Alex also argues that Stan "shoved me in a washing machine in my own house." Stan notices Alex and confronts him, "Hey Twinkle Douche. If I wanted you in the cafeteria, I would've taped you to a lunch lady. Mike steps in and challenges Stan who wants to know what Mike is going to do. "First, I'm gonna call your father." Stan throws the ball at Mike's face, who catches it with one hand. Mike adds, "Stan, I feel sorry for you. You're the man—captain of the basketball team. Dates the pretty girls. High school is your kingdom. But, people, Stan's a bully. Why? It'd be way too easy to say Stan preys on the weak simply because he's a dick. No. No. No. Stan here is much more complex than that. See, according to leading psychiatrists, Stan's a bully for one of three reasons. One: underneath all that male bravado there's an insecure little girl banging on the closet door trying to get out. Two: like a caveman, Stan's brain is underdeveloped. Therefore, Stan is unable to use self-control. And so he acts out aggressively. And the third reason: Stan has a small weiner." The scene ends after Mike performs some basketball moves and tells Stan, "Don't hurt yourself, big boy."

> *17 Again* (New Line, 2009), written by Jason Filardi and directed by Burr Steers
> **Elapsed Time:** This scene begins at 37:01 and ends at 40:13
> **Rating:** Rated PG-13 for language, some sexual material and teen partying

About a Boy   HARASSMENT
Will Freeman (Hugh Grant) is an immature man approaching middle age. A young boy teaches him what it means to be a grown-up.

Marcus approaches his friends Nicky and Mark during recess. Soon, two older boys start kicking a ball at them and insulting them. The ball hits one of the boys and bounces away. The boy blames them for making him lose his football. Mark tells Marcus "we don't really want you hanging around with us anymore." He cites "It's because of them. We never used to have any trouble before we started hanging around with you. Now we get it every single day. Besides, everyone thinks you're weird. The scene ends as Marcus walks away narrating his position, "There you have it. I was having a shit time at home and at school."

> *About a Boy* (Universal, 2002), written Peter Hedges and directed by Chris Weitz, Paul Weitz
> **Elapsed Time:** This scene begins at 12:11 and ends at 13:21
> **Rating:** Rated PG-13 for brief strong language and some thematic elements

Accepted   HAZING/HUMILIATION
Barnaby and his friends create a fake university when none of them are accepted into real colleges. How long can they fool their parents and the government in the legitimacy of their venture?

Schrader (Jonah Hill) is attempting to pledge his dream fraternity. He is dressed in a sperm costume and holding a tray of cups. One of the fraternity brothers invites him to take a drink, but another brother halts him and spits in the glass. Schrader complements, "Good addition, sir" and takes a drink. The fraternity boys laugh as the scene ends.

> *Accepted* (Universal, 2006), written by Adam Cooper and directed by Steve Pink
> **Elapsed Time:** This scene begins at 51:28 and ends at 51:50
> **Rating:** Rated PG-13 for language, sexual material, and drug content

Agent Cody Banks   REVENGE
Cody (Frankie Muniz) is selected for a highly trained government program that needs younger employees.

Cody (Frankie Muniz) is undercover as a high school student. He enters the chemistry class where he runs into Natalie Conners (Hillary Duff), the person he is assigned to follow. He is mesmerized by her and inadvertently walks into a crowd of boys. They address him as "new kid—the scholarship case from the other side of town." As he tries to leave, Cody's watch is taken by one of the boys. The boy dares him to do something about it. In a dream sequence, Cody quickly dispatches him. In real life, Cody tells him, "If you're going to keep my watch, promise me you won't touch that silver button." The boy promptly touches it and is electrocuted. The scene ends as Cody declares, "I told you not to touch it."

> *Agent Cody Banks* (MGM, 2003), written by Ashley Miller and directed by Harald Zwart
> **Elapsed Time:** This scene begins at 22:38 and ends at 24:06
> **Rating:** Rated PG for action violence, mild language and some sensual content

American Bully   PHYSICAL/HARASSMENT/BIAS
A middle-eastern teenage boy who is affected by 9/11, terrorism, and the war in Iraq becomes involved in an isolated high school altercation that escalates into a hate crime that shocks the entire nation.

Brandon and Bo arrive at a local convenience store to purchase beer. They recognize the store clerk, Eric, as the one who got them in trouble at school. Bo asks, "where's the cheese at, rat?" Eric tells the boys that he cannot sell them beer (despite Brandon's attempt to use a fake ID). Brandon charges "Sell us this beer since you got me suspended today." The duo continue to taunt Eric and curse at him until a police car shows up outside.

> *American Bully* (MGM, 2003), written by Zak Meyers & Dave Rodriguez and directed by Dave Rodriguez
> **Elapsed Time:** This scene begins at 31:28 and ends at 33:26
> **Rating:** Rated R for disturbing violent content, a scene of sexuality, drinking, drug use and pervasive language—all involving teens

American Bully   PHYSICAL/HARASSMENT/DISCRIMINATION

A middle-eastern teenage boy who is affected by 9/11, terrorism, and the war in Iraq becomes involved in an isolated high school altercation that escalates into a hate crime that shocks the entire nation.

Brandon, Bo, and Mike are driving down the street the evening following Brandon's suspension. They happen upon Eric who is walking down the street. Brandon asks "Where's the principal and the cop now to save your ass, huh?" Eric angrily returns "Hey, fuck you, you redneck pieces of shit" and runs away. Bo and Brandon chase him on foot. When they catch him, they physically assault Eric and drag him back to the car amid Eric's screams. The scene ends as Mike drives down the street as Brandon declares, "Hurry up, Mike, I'm getting a little antsy!"

> *American Bully* (MGM, 2003), written by Zak Meyers & Dave Rodriguez and directed by Dave Rodriguez
> **Elapsed Time:** This scene begins at 41:15 and ends at 43:40
> **Rating:** Rated R for disturbing violent content, a scene of sexuality, drinking, drug use and pervasive language—all involving teens

American Bully   PHYSICAL/HARASSMENT/DISCRIMINATION

A middle-eastern teenage boy who is affected by 9/11, terrorism, and the war in Iraq becomes involved in an isolated high school altercation that escalates into a hate crime that shocks the entire nation.

Brandon, Bo, and Mike drag an unconscious Eric into an abandoned house. They begin to bind his hands and feet with duct tape, "I don't want there to be circulation." All along, Eric screams for help. Brandon punches Eric in the face.

Bo pours beer onto Eric's face "This right here is for all our people this motherfucker killed." Brandon cocks a shotgun into Eric's face. "Right now," Brandon consoles, "you need to come to terms with the fact we're going to torture you just like your people do to Americans." The scene ends when Mike goes to the car to search for his cigarettes.

> *American Bully* (MGM, 2003), written by Zak Meyers & Dave Rodriguez and directed by Dave Rodriguez
> **Elapsed Time:** This scene begins at 44:56 and ends at 48:25
> **Rating:** Rated R for disturbing violent content, a scene of sexuality, drinking, drug use and pervasive language—all involving teens

American Teen   CYBERBULLYING

Documents the life of high school teens in a small Indiana town.

The scene begins as a boy narrates how Erica sent him a picture of herself topless. He admits sending it to a few friends via email. Those friends continue to forward the email to others in the school. Later, a group of students are discussing the picture. A boy admits "It was a joke. I don't even think it should have been sent to anyone in the first place...stupid." Megan asks for Erica's number and leaves a disguised message "Not only are you a slut, but you're also dumb. I've seen your titties, and so has everyone else. Your parents know. Your priest knows. And above all, God knows. I hate to be the bearer of bad news, but you're sentenced to be a slut for the rest of your life." Another girl calls back. Disguising her voice, she adds "Like, oh my gosh, I was online today looking at natty ho's, and your picture popped up, and you were, like, topless, and I thought, 'Who the hell would put a natty picture of themselves like that online, when your body is not even that nice and your tits are not even that nice?'" A boy asks, "What if she kills herself in the morning?" Megan returns "She won't. We'll leave her a message telling her not to kill herself, that life will get better." The scene ends as Erica sits in a school lounge and admits "It's been hard."

> *American Teen* (57th and Irving Productions, 2008), written and directed by Nanette Burstein
> **Elapsed Time:** This scene begins at 25:54 and ends at 29:04
> **Rating:** Rated PG-13 for some strong language, sexual material, some drinking and brief smoking-all involving teens

Andre   SOCIAL EXCLUSION

A young girl befriends and adopts a loveable sea lion named Andre.

As Toni (Tina Majorino) enters the classroom, a group of young girls beckon for her to join them. Once cajoled to the gathering, the group leader begins to show off her ring that her paramour had given her. She invites Toni to take a closer look, and when she does, she gets sprayed in the face with water. The others laugh as the teacher calls everyone to attention. Toni wipes tears from her eyes as the scene ends.

> *Andre* (Paramount, 1994), written by Dana Baratta and directed by George Miller
> **Elapsed Time:** This scene begins at 6:05 and ends at 7:15
> **Rating:** Rated PG for teen mischief, mild violence and language

Anger Management   PHYSICAL/HUMILIATION
Dave Buznik (Adam Sandler) is mandated to attend court-ordered anger management therapy. His therapist (Jack Nicholson), however, is a bit of a loose cannon himself.

At the beginning of the film, young Dave Buznik sits on the sidewalk at a neighborhood block party. He is mooning over a young Sara Paulson. The two appear to be hitting it off and Sara challenges Dave to kiss her. The two pucker up and are leaning in when suddenly Dave's gym shorts and underwear are torn down. As partiers laugh [at the size of Dave's penis], the voice of the perpetrator taunts "Got any mustard for that cocktail frank, butt-lick."

> *Anger Management* (Revolution Studios, 2003), written by David Dorfman and directed by Peter Segal
> **Elapsed Time:** This scene begins at 0:57 and ends at 2:42
> **Rating:** Rated PG-13 on appeal for crude sexual content and language

Anger Management   PHYSICAL/REVENGE
Dave Buznik (Adam Sandler) is mandated to attend court-ordered anger management therapy. His therapist (Jack Nicholson), however, is a bit of a loose cannon himself.

David Buznik (Adam Sandler) is being forced by his therapist, Dr. Buddy Rydell (Jack Nicholson) to confront his childhood bully who is now a practicing monk. The duo find Arnie Shenkman (John C. Reilly) (who now identifies as Pana Kamanana) praying at a monastery. Dave asks Buddy. "You want me to fight a monk? He's not even allowed to hurt a plant." Buddy responds, "For Pete's sake, this is the monk that twisted your tits! Confront him or you're going to prison!" Arnie admits that he was a "cretin" towards Dave and begins to list some of the ways he mistreated Dave. When Dave adds that Arnie pulled Dave's pants down in front of Sarah Paulson, Arnie chuckles, "That actually was pretty funny." Their exchanges turns physical as Dave begins to insult Arnie's mentally ill sister. Dave overpowers Arnie and gives him a wedgie. The scene ends as the other monks chase Dave and Buddy away.

Anger Management (Revolution Studios, 2003), written by David Dorfman and directed by Peter Segal
Elapsed Time: This scene begins at 6:03and ends at 11:13
Rating: Rated PG-13 on appeal for crude sexual content and language

Benchwarmers, The   PHYSICAL/BYSTANDER
Three grown men with a childhood chip on their shoulders decide to take on all little league challengers in three-man baseball. They become the champions for all wannabes and social outcasts.

Three socially inept young children are playing baseball in the local park when members of the organized little league team try to force them off the diamond. One of the young kids argues that the team's practice does not start until 4:30; the team leader states "We want to have a practice before the practice." A girl who was with the original group suggests they all play together when an older boy retorts "No, because you suck. Why don't you go home and build your science projects." The oldest boy pushes the other boy down, and while another team member holds him, the oldest nearly sits on the boy's face and gives him some "beef stew" (he farted just above his nose). The young boy is rescued when an adult named Gus (played by Ron Schneider) chases the older boys away. In tears, the young boy tells Gus, "It actually didn't taste as bad as you'd think" and runs away. Gus ponders, "Why do kids have to be so fricking cruel?"

The Benchwarmers (Revolution Studios, 2006), written by Allen Covert & Nick Swardson and directed by Dennis Dugan
Elapsed Time: This scene begins at:50 and ends at 4:04
Rating: Rated PG-13 for crude and suggestive humor, and for language

Boy Next Door, The BYSTANDER
Claire Peterson (Jennifer Lopez) does the unthinkable and beds the young boy living next door. The affair takes a dangerous turn when she tries to call it off.

Kevin Peterson is getting some things from his school locker when he is approached by Jason Zimmer and his crew of friends. Jason tells Kevin he saw Kevin's movie *The Wiz* on television (referencing a past time when Kevin peed his pants in school). Kevin slams his locker, "Fuck you, Zimmer!" As Jason approaches Kevin, Noah Sandborn intervenes and violently assaults Jason. A teacher, Miss Lansing (Chrisen Chenowith) stops the fight as Noah bangs Jason's head off the locker.

> *The Boy Next Door* (Universal, 2015), written by Barbara Curry and directed by Rob Cohen
> **Elapsed Time:** This scene begins at 47:23 and ends at 48:14
> **Rating:** Rated R for violence, sexual content/nudity and language

Boy Next Door, The VERBAL
Claire Peterson (Jennifer Lopez) does the unthinkable and beds the young boy living next door. The affair takes a dangerous turn when she tries to call it off.

Kevin and Noah are at the hardware store when they notice Kevin's crush, Allie Peterson, working the cash register. Kevin asks Noah to purchase the items because she is "The most beautiful girl at school, and I just can't think when I'm around her." Allie and Kevin are talking when Jason and crew enter the store. They begin taunting Kevin. Jason wonders if the small pouch Jason is carrying is "your little penis purse?" Allie throws the boys from the store.

> *The Boy Next Door* (Universal, 2015), written by Barbara Curry and directed by Rob Cohen
> **Elapsed Time:** This scene begins at 6:43 and ends at 8:35
> **Rating:** Rated R for violence, sexual content/nudity and language

Bridge to Terabithia VERBAL/INTIMIDATION
The classic children's story by Katherine Paterson comes to life in this literary adaptation. Jesse has been training all year long to be the fastest boy in the 5th grade relay races. He manages to beat everyone except Leslie, a new girl who blows

THE BIG SHORT 71

past him. The two forge an unlikely friendship and together rule an imaginary world of their creation.

May Belle is excited that her dad packed Twinkies in her lunch and she is announcing this to her friends on the school playground. Looking over his shoulder, her older brother, Jess, warns her to stop bragging about the dessert. She argues back, "You're just mad because I got some and you didn't." Jess states that he just doesn't want her to lose the cakes. Soon, May Belle comes running to tell Jess that the school bully, Janice, has stolen her Twinkies. Several other young students are complaining that Janice also makes them pay one dollar to use the bathroom. In the background, Janice is blocking the bathroom door. Jess's friend, Leslie, leads a protest march towards the bathroom while chanting "Free the pee" because "That's not fair. Peeing's definitely supposed to be free." May Belle confronts Janice about the stolen cakes and demands that she return them. When Janice refuses, May Belle tells Jess "You're supposed to beat her up. You're my brother." Fearful, Jess tells May Belle "Do you know what would happen if I were to pick a fight with her?" to which May Belle answers, "You'll get your butt kicked." May Belle walks away crying. Leslie tells her, "We'll get her back, won't we Jess?"

Bridge to Terabithia (Walt Disney Pictures and Walden Media, 2007), written by Jeff Stockwell and David Patterson, directed by Gabor Csupo
Elapsed Time: This scene begins at 41:13 and ends at 42:50
Rating: Rated PG for thematic elements including bullying, some peril and mild language

Brotherhood, The   HAZING/HUMILIATION
The Doma Tau Omega fraternity is searching for new recruits. How will being vampires affect their recruitment efforts?

A young man and lady are kissing in his bedroom. He asks permission to put his hand between her legs. She consents. Outside the room, several young men have gathered and are talking about the goings-on. One questions, "Did you guys see her?" Another answers, "She wasn't *that* big." Another adds, "I don't know about that one. She was pretty damn big!" Soon, the amorous man grabs the young lady and yelps aloud. The other men come rushing into the room. The young woman screams for the men to "get out of here" while keeping her nudity covered. The room is filled by this time and each boy tries to push the woman back onto the bed. The ringleader pulls the young man from the bed and several others drag him and place him into the trunk of a car and give him several bottles of alcohol. "Don't you ever treat a woman like that again in this house! Where'd you learn that shit, huh? That is detestable! Now, you're gonna stay in here and you're gonna finish all these before you can get out. That's your punishment, bitch!" They slam the trunk closed to end the scene.

> ***The Brotherhood*** (Hunting Lane Films, 2010), written by Will Canon & Doug Simon and directed by Will Canon
> **Elapsed Time:** This scene begins at 14:24 and 16:21
> **Rating:** Rated R for pervasive language, some violence and sexual content

Buried Alive   HAZING/HUMILIATION
A college sorority awakens a killer spirit during a sorority ritual.

Rene and Zane have arrived to pick up a couple of sorority pledges. Zane wonders how they will find the two girls. Rene says they'll stand out. The duo discover the pledges dressed in animal costumes. Upon seeing them, Phil declares "that is awesome! It's humiliating!" Zane adds "I think the spark of sadism definitely has your fingerprints on it, cuz." The girls are brandishing signs that correspond to their costumes "I'd be a cow for Omega Tau" and "I would bow wow for Omega Tau." The young ladies wonder where the group is going. Rene responds "All you two need to know is that, wherever we go, you're my servants, my slaves." Erin questions, "What exactly does this initiation consist of?" Rene answers, "Whatever comes to mind." "And what a mind she has," Zane adds, "I'd be afraid girls. She's really good at mental cruelty. But she's not above a little physical abuse either."

> ***Buried Alive*** (Horror Two, 2007), written by Art Monterastelli and directed by Robert Kurtzman
> **Elapsed Time:** This scene begins at 11:40 and ends at 13:32
> **Rating:** Rated R

Can't Hardly Wait   REVENGE
Desperate to lose their virginity before they graduate high school, three friends make big plans for an adventure-filled night.

William Lichter declares "Mike Dexter is an asshole! For the past decade, he has made a hobby of my pain." He explains how Mike destroyed his 8th grade science

THE BIG SHORT 73

project and other ways he humiliated the teen. "Well, gentlemen, tonight Mike Dexter will know humiliation. Tonight, Mike Dexter will know ridicule. Tonight is the night we fight back. Tonight is our independence night!" William reviews the plans for retaliation. "Now, I will lead Mike and one of his random jock friends behind the pool house to here and here where you two will be waiting. You jump down on them, rendering them unconscious with the chloroform that we mixed in chem lab. Then we strip off said jocks' clothes and take Polaroids of them in a lurid, naked embrace. The boys exit the basement to end the scene.

> *Can't Hardly Wait* (Columbia Pictures, 1998), written and by Deborah Kaplan & Harry Elfont
> **Elapsed Time:** This scene begins at 7:35 and ends at 9:41
> **Rating:** Rated PG-13 for teen drinking and sexuality, and for language

Carrie   HUMILIATION
Stephen King's classic take follows Carrie White, a social misfit who learns she has telekinetic powers.

Carrie White is taking a shower when she sees blood pouring down her legs. She panics and runs naked from the shower screaming for assistance from other students. The girls laugh and hang tampons and throw maxipads at her taunting "Plug it up!" Carrie's teacher intervenes and tries to calm Carrie down.

> *Carrie* (Red Bank Films, 1976), written by Stephen King & Lawrence D. Cohen and directed by Brian De Palma
> **Elapsed Time:** This scene begins at 3:49 and ends at 6:09
> **Rating:** Rated R

Carrie   PHYSICAL/REVENGE
Stephen King's classic take follows Carrie White, a social misfit who learns she has telekinetic powers.

Carrie and Tommy have just been elected king and queen of the prom. They approach the stage to the adulation of many at the prom. They are unaware that Cindy and others have plotted to embarrass her by spilling pig's blood on the couple. The bucket hits Tommy in the head and knocks him unconscious. Using her telekinetic powers, Carrie annihilates the students as they run from the building.

> *Carrie* (Red Bank Films, 1976), written by Stephen King & Lawrence D. Cohen and directed by Brian De Palma
> **Elapsed Time:** This scene begins at 1:10:09 and ends at 1:19:15
> **Rating:** Rated R

Central Intelligence   HUMILIATION/BYSTANDER

Kevin Hart stars as Calvin Joyner. When Calvin was in high school, he was a superstar. He befriended social outcast Robbie Weirdicht (Dwayne Johnson). Twenty years later, Robbie now goes by Bob Stone and is a superspy on the run from the CIA. He enlists Calvin for help and the duo set out to clear Bob's name.

The film starts off during first period at Central High School. Robbie is taking a shower in the locker room. Meanwhile, a large assembly is convening in the gymnasium where Calvin has been named "Student of the Year." Robbie is dancing and singing in the shower when he is accosted by a group of young men. They boys toss his naked body into the gymnasium as the ringleader shouts "Check out my weird dick!" The audience erupts in laughter and pointed fingers. Calvin gives his jacket to cover his nakedness and to allow Robbie to exit gracefully. Principal Kent (Phil Reeves) walks up to Calvin and states, "Well, there's no coming back from that."

> *Central Inteligence* (New Line Cinema, 2016), written by Gustin Nash and directed by Rawson Marshall Thurber
> **Elapsed Time:** This scene begins at 1:03 and ends at 5:13
> **Rating:** Rated PG-13 for crude and suggestive humor, some nudity, action violence and brief strong language

Charlie Bartlett   PHYSICAL

Rich boy Charlie (Anton Yelchin) is transplanted to a public high school and learns to fit in by becoming a pharmaceutical drug dealer.

Charlie is being beaten by an older student named Murphy. "I'm gonna fuck you up!" He pauses to make sure his friend is recording the beating via video. Murph asks Charlie, "How does that feel? I don't care. You know why? Because that was a rhetorical question." The recording boy asks, "Hey, Charlie, what's Latin for 'I'm a total pussy?'" The boys leave an injured Charlie on the hallway floor.

> *Charlie Bartlett* (MGM, 2007), written by Ike Barinholtz & David Stassen and directed by Jon Poll
> Elapsed Time: This scene begins at 13:10 and ends at 13:33
> Rating: Rated R for language, drug content and brief nudity

Charlie Bartlett PHYSICAL
Rich boy Charlie (Anton Yelchin) is transplanted to a public high school and learns to fit in by becoming a pharmaceutical drug dealer.

Charlie enters the restroom as Murphy and friend are conducting business [selling drugs]. "Just fucking buy it. You've done it every other time." The duo tease Charlie for carrying an attache case and a sport jacket. "Is he, like, a total faggot or what?" When Charlie asks if that question was rhetorical, Murph grabs him and plunges Charlie's head into the toilet. "Fuck him up!" Murph charges, "Guess what? I think you like that, you little bitch." A teacher's entrance breaks up the ruckus. Murph says, "Later, homo" as he exits.

> *Charlie Bartlett* (MGM, 2007), written by Gustin Nash and directed by Jon Poll
> Elapsed Time: This scene begins at 8:51 and ends at 10:24
> Rating: Rated R for language, drug content and brief nudity

Christmas Story, A PHYSICAL/INTIMIDATION
As Christmas nears, all Ralphie can think about is getting a new BB gun. His parents are convinced he is going to shoot his eye out.

Ralphie (Peter Billingsley) and his friends are walking home from school and discussing the day's excitement. Soon, they hear the familiar laugh of Scut Farkus, their feared nemesis. After Scut pushes Randy (Ian Petrella) down, he then roars and scares Ralphie and crew, who run in the opposite direction. They are scared back by Grover Dill, "Farkus' crummy little toady. Mean. Rotten. His lips curled over his green teeth." Farkus grabs Schwartz and wrenches his arm behind him until Scwartz cries out "Uncle!" Ralph (voiced as an adult) narrates "In our world, you were either a bully, a toady, or one of the nameless rabble of victims." The scene ends after the boys run away and the bullies walk in a separate direction.

A Christmas Story (MGM, 1983), written by Jean Shepherd and directed by Bob Clark
Elapsed Time: This scene begins at 21:50 and ends at 23:59
Rating: Rated PG

Chronicle   PHYSICAL
After finding an underground artifact from outer space, three teens realize they now have superpowers. As they learn to use their powers, the world spins out of control.

Andrew Detmer (Dane DeHaan) is filming the daily goings-on in his high school. He is standing near his locker when a couple of goons accost him. One of them put him in a headlock and repeatedly slaps him and taunts him asking "You gonna cry?" Andrew asks them to return his camera. "Huh? You want your camera? Piece of shit from, like, 2004?" Before leaving him alone, the boys slide Andrew's camera on the floor back to Andrew. Andrew calls them "assholes" as they depart.

Chronicle (20th Century Fox, 2012), written by Max Landis and directed by Josh Trank
Elapsed Time: This scene begins at 4:30 and ends at 5:02
Rating: Rated PG-13 for intense action and violence, thematic material, some language, sexual content and teen drinking

Clique, The   SOCIAL EXCLUSION
Massie is the daughter of a servant to a rich family. She would give anything to fit in with the high society folks. That is, until she befriends Alicia, the queen bee.

Massie Block (Elizabeth McLaughlin) is standing at the doorway of the cafeteria. She has just returned from obtaining a new jacket from the school's lost-and-found. Several young ladies see her. Alicia (Samantha Boscarino) remarks, "Looks like someone went shopping at Nursestrom's today [the lost & found is located in the nurse's office]." She begins chanting "Loser, loser, double loser, whatever, as if, get the picture, duh" as the other girls join in.

The Clique (Alloy Entertainment, 2008), written by Liz Tigelaar and directed by Michael Lembeck
Elapsed Time: This scene begins at 26:14 and ends at 27:00
Rating: Rated PG for thematic material, rude behavior and language

College   PHYSICAL/HAZING

On an admissions open house weekend, three high school students hope to fulfill their lecherous desires by attending parties, drinking, and having sex at college. Pretending to be college freshmen, the lads attend rush activities at a banned fraternity house. They get much more than what they planned for.

Thinking they are going to do body shots off willing sorority women, the boys are duped into participating in a hazing ritual by the brothers of the fraternity. The trio is shocked to see that they will actually be doing body shots off a naked, hairy Bearcat (Gary Owens). As they display displeasure in the prospect, Teague (Nick Zano), the fraternity leader, shouts, "That's right, motherfuckers!" The boys are barred from leaving. Teague states, "Yeah, we thought you guys were cool. We thought you wanted to party. Guess we were wrong. Well, have fun back at the dorm, you fucking pussies." Soon, the boys reluctantly participate in the drinking activities, including drinking alcohol poured through Bearcat's hairy butt crack.

> *College* (Element Films, 2008), written by Dan Callahan & Adam Ellison and directed Deb Hagan
> **Elapsed Time:** This scene begins at 23:46 and ends at 26:30
> **Rating:** Rated R for pervasive crude and sexual content, nudity, language, drug and alcohol abuse

College   PHYSICAL/HAZING

On an admissions open house weekend, three high school students hope to fulfill their lecherous desires by attending parties, drinking, and having sex at college. Pretending to be college freshmen, the lads attend rush activities at a banned fraternity house. They get much more than what they planned for.

The boys are walking across campus when suddenly a water balloon hits Kevin (Drake Bell) in the side of the head. Teague states, "Don't worry! That was not full of my piss or anything…Just Bearcat's." Teague questions if the boys had enjoyed the party they were sent to (at a gay fraternity). One of the brothers mimics receiving oral sex. Carter (Andrew Caldwell) complains but is interrupted by Bearcat, "Watch your step, pre-frosh! This ain't high school!" Teague answers, "Welcome to college, boys. Enjoy!"

> *College* (Element Films, 2008), written by Dan Callahan & Adam Ellison and directed Deb Hagan
> **Elapsed Time:** This scene begins at 21:51 and ends at 22:15
> **Rating:** Rated R for pervasive crude and sexual content, nudity, language, drug and alcohol abuse

Contest   PHYSICAL
Tommy Dolen (Danny Flaherty) is often bullied. When he is suddenly befriended by his bully, Matt Prylek (Kenton Duty), he isn't sure of what to do.

Tommy (Danny Flaherty) is sitting alone in the school cafeteria. Soon, Joe (Alex Boniello) and his crew approach Tommy. Joe invites Tommy to go to the TV station then grabs Tommy's head and slams it onto the table. Matt punches Joe in the stomach and he and Tommy walk away. When Joe recovers, he saves face by stating "Matt and I may join drama club" and takes a bow.

> *Contest* (Contest LLC, 2013), written and directed by Anthony Joseph Giunta
> **Elapsed Time:** This scene begins at 14:03 and ends at 15:40
> **Rating:** Rated PG for some bullying, rude humor and language

Contest   PHYSICAL
Tommy Dolen (Danny Flaherty) is often bullied. When he is suddenly befriended by his bully, Matt Prylek (Kenton Duty), he isn't sure of what to do.

In a voiceover, Tommy narrates how he's bullied by the swim team as they forcibly carry him from the locker room to throw him into the pool. The school's camera surveillance records the affair as Matt dives in to save him.

> *Contest* (Contest LLC, 2013), written and directed by Anthony Joseph Giunta
> **Elapsed Time:** This scene begins at 0:17 and ends at 1:19
> **Rating:** Rated PG for some bullying, rude humor and language

Craft, The   SOCIAL EXCLUSION/VERBAL/DISCRIMATION
A group of friends use witchcraft to settle the score with anyone and everyone who has ever done them wrong, but will the "magic" take them too far? What happens when they turn on each other?

Laura (Christine Taylor) has made it her mission to make Rochelle's (Rachel True) life a living hell. She is in the bathroom talking to some other girls while Rochelle is listening on the other side of the wall. She begins by complaining "there's a pubic hair on my brush. Oh no, wait. That's just one of Rochelle's little nappy hairs." Rochelle comes around the corner to ask why Laura keeps making fun of her. Her answer was simple, "Because I don't like Negroids. Sorry." Laura and her friends laugh and walk out the door.

> *The Craft* (Bob Yari Productions, 2004), written and directed by Paul Haggis
> Elapsed Time: This scene begins at 00:23:56 and ends at 00:24:40
> Rating: R for language, sexual content, and some violence

Cursed   **PHYSICAL/HARASSMENT**

Horror master Wes Craven satisfies the bloodlust in all of us as Ellie (Christina Ricci) and her brother, Jimmy, learn that they have been infected and are changing into werewolves. The Los Angeles night life just got a little more interesting!

Jimmy (Jesse Eisenberg) comes upon his lost dog, Zipper, as he has wandered into the cinema where Brooke (Kristina Anapau) works. They are interrupted by Bo (Milo Ventimiglia), Brooke's boyfriend, who taunts Jimmy as "the dodgeball crotch target." Bo adds, "I'm just looking out for him. He can't help it. Every school's got one—the derogatory 'it.' A geek on his way to fag town." Jimmy defends, "I'm not gay," Bo responds, "Bummer. You mean you're just an ass wimp-wad for no reason?" Brooke tells Bo "You're such a dick" and tells Jimmy to ignore him. As Jimmy departs, Bo adds, "I think your dog is gay too."

> *Cursed* (Dimension Films, 2005), written by Kevin Williamson and directed by Wes Craven
> Elapsed Time: This scene begins at 2:39 and ends at 4:29
> Rating: Rated PG-13 for horror violence/terror, some sexual references, nudity, language and a brief drug reference

Cursed   **PHYSICAL/AGGRESSION/INTIMIDATION/BIAS**

Horror master Wes Craven satisfies the bloodlust in all of us as Ellie (Christina Ricci) and her brother, Jimmy, learn that they have been infected and are changing into werewolves. The Los Angeles night life just got a little more interesting!

Jimmy (Jesse Eisenberg) offers Brooke some change when she's having difficulty getting the soda machine to take her dollar. Bo intervenes and knocks Jimmy's books from his hands. He asks Jimmy if he plans to try out for the wrestling team. Jimmy answers, "Oh, no. I don't wrestle." Bo retorts, "Oh, I'd think all that male to male contact would be right up your alley." Jimmy wonders, "Is that the appeal for you?" Bo wonders, "Did you just attempt a confrontation?" Brooke drags Bo away; As they depart, Bo pushes Jimmy and Bo tells his friends, "Let's get out of here before we get homo stained."

> *Cursed* (Dimension Films, 2005), written by Kevin Williamson and directed by Wes Craven
> **Elapsed Time:** This scene begins at 26:01 and ends at 27:24
> **Rating:** Rated PG-13 for horror violence/terror, some sexual references, nudity, language and a brief drug reference

Cursed　　　　　　　　　　　　　　　　　　**VERBAL/HARASSMENT/BIAS**
Horror master Wes Craven satisfies the bloodlust in all of us as Ellie (Christina Ricci) and her brother, Jimmy, learn that they have been infected and are changing into werewolves. The Los Angeles night life just got a little more interesting!

Brooke and her friends are watching the wrestling team's practice. When Bo notices her talking to Jummy, he questions, "Are you going fruit fly on me?" Jimmy tells Bo to "Shoo." Jimmy tells Bo he is becoming transparent "Cause all this internalized homophobia's giving you away." Bo pushes Jimmy and warns him, "You better watch your ass." The wrestling coach intervenes and soon Jimmy is trying out for the wrestling team. His sparring partner quips, "OK, limp wrist, stay away from my groin." Bo joins in as Jimmy bests the other student. He taunts Jimmy by calling him a "fairy" and a "fag." The scene ends as Jimmy suplexes Bo onto the mat amid cheers from those watching.

> *Cursed* (Dimension Films, 2005), written by Kevin Williamson and directed by Wes Craven
> **Elapsed Time:** This scene begins at 43:06 and ends at 46:50
> **Rating:** Rated PG-13 for horror violence/terror, some sexual references, nudity, language and a brief drug reference

Cyberbully   **CYBERBULLYING**
Taylor (Emily Osment) realizes she is the target of several of her peers bullying attacks. They torment her by disgracing her online.

Taylor (Emily Osment) rushes into her house after school. She is visibly upset as her mother, Kris (Kelly Rowan) attempts to talk to her. A parent calls to tell her what happened to Taylor. The scene switches to Taylor looking at the negative comments on her social media page. Kris chides Taylor for not shutting down her page and orders her to close it. Taylor reads a new message exclaiming "Look, mom, I'm so popular" and reads the comment aloud before slamming her laptop closed.

> *Cyberbully* (Muse Entertainment, 2011), written by Teena Booth and directed by Charles Biname
> **Elapsed Time:** This scene begins at 32:10 and ends at 34:17
> **Rating:** Rated TV-14

Cyberbully   **CYBERBULLYING**
Taylor (Emily Osment) realizes she is the target of several of her peers bullying attacks. They torment her by disgracing her online.

Taylor is told about a video of her being circulated online. She opens her laptop to find that someone has posted a fake video soliciting a boy for money. The masked girl mimics, "I act like I'm the most holy and pure thing at school, but I'm really the dirtiest, little whore!" Taylor cries and pushes the laptop away.

> *Cyberbully* (Muse Entertainment, 2011), written by Teena Booth and directed by Charles Biname
> **Elapsed Time:** This scene begins at 40:27 and ends at 43:02
> **Rating:** Rated TV-14

D3: The Mighty Ducks   **INTIMIDATION/HARASSMENT**
The freshmen hockey team are taking heat from the varsity players. Can they prove themselves?

The freshmen hockey team has been chastised by their coach. As they're undressing out of their uniforms, they realize their clothes are missing. They find that their clothes have been burned and are in the shower. Someone has scrawled "Freshmen stink" on the shower wall with shaving cream.

> *D3: The Mighty Ducks* (Walt Disney Pictures, 1996), written by Steven Brill & Jim Burnstein and directed by Robert Lieberman
> **Elapsed Time:** This scene begins at 42:47 and ends at 43:13
> **Rating:** Rated PG for some hockey rough-housing and mild language

D3: The Mighty Ducks   INTIMIDATION/REVENGE

The freshmen hockey team are taking heat from the varsity players. Can they prove themselves?

Cole (Michael Cudlitz) has taken a younger student's lunch and is passing the contents to his friends. Charlie (Josh Jackson) and his friends devise a plan to get back at the jocks. They put horse manure in a lunch bag. Cole steals the lunch bag and finds the horse turds and chases the students from the cafeteria.

> *D3: The Mighty Ducks* (Walt Disney Pictures, 1996), written by Steven Brill & Jim Burnstein and directed by Robert Lieberman
> **Elapsed Time:** This scene begins at 22:34 and ends at 26:13
> **Rating:** Rated PG for some hockey rough-housing and mild language

D3: The Mighty Ducks   PHYSICAL/INTIMIDATION

The freshmen hockey team are taking heat from the varsity players. Can they prove themselves?

A young male student follows Connie (Marguerite Moreau) as she walks down the school hallway. An older athlete wonders, "What's he looking at?" Cole follows and soon pushes the lad into the lockers and then steal a kid's lunch because "All this work makes me hungry."

> *D3: The Mighty Ducks* (Walt Disney Pictures, 1996), written by Steven Brill & Jim Burnstein and directed by Robert Lieberman
> **Elapsed Time:** This scene begins at 12:43 and ends at 13:07
> **Rating:** Rated PG for some hockey rough-housing and mild language

Dazed and Confused   PHYSICAL/HAZING/HARASSMENT

It's the last day of school and the seniors wreak havoc on the lives of freshmen and upcoming middle schoolers.

It's the last day of school and the students are trashing the school as they depart. Several seniors carrying paddles hunt freshmen students to punish. The scene cuts to several young girls being forced into pickup trucks and given pacifiers to suck. The senior girls gather up the freshmen girls and make them perform air raid drills in the parking lot. The freshmen are referred to as "bitches" and "sluts" while the seniors pour ketchup, mustard, eggs, and flour on them.

> *Dazed & Confused* (Gramercy Pictures, 1993), written and directed by Richard Linklater
> **Elapsed Time:** This scene begins at 15:29 and ends at 24:10
> **Rating:** Rated R for pervasive, continuous teen drug and alcohol use and very strong language

Diary of a Wimpy Kid   INTIMIDATION/PHYSICAL

Greg (Zachary Gordon) narrates his life with his parents and mean older brother while learning to navigate middle school.

Although Greg (Zachary Gordon) and Rowley (Robert Capron) are best friends, they are somehow goaded into fighting each other. As they grapple, Pete (Nicholas Carey) and Carter (Samuel Patrick Chu), two known bullies, pull up in their truck. They interrupt Greg and Rowley's squabble, "Well, well, well, look who we have here. You're so freaking dead." Pete disperses the onlooking crowd by yelling "All you guys better scram or I'm gonna kick your butts, too!" Greg and Rowley try to run away too, but they are caught. Pete threatens "You guys have no idea what I'm gonna do to you." Carter questions, "What are we gonna do?" Noticing the rotten, moldy piece of cheese on the playground, Pete states, "I know what we're gonna do. Give me the wide one [referring to Rowley]." Pete tells Rowley to eat the cheese "or I'll shove the entire thing down your throat." When the children return to view the goings-on, Greg tells everyone that he ate the cheese to defend Rowley. "I ate the cheese. And you know what people? I just did you all a huge favor. I ate the cheese to show you all how stupid this whole school is. The wrong friends. The wrong lunch table. The wrong butt? It's all meaningless. Just like this cheese. I know it. You all know it. So come on. Everyone else who's sick of it, step forward and join me!"

Patty Farrell (Laine Macneil) yells out "Greg Heffley has the Cheese Touch!" and the children scatter in fear.

> *Diary of a Wimpy Kid* (Color Force, 2010), written by Jackie Filgo & Jeff Filgo and directed by Thor Freudenthal
> **Elapsed Time:** This scene begins at 1:20:40 and ends at 1:24:32
> **Rating:** Rated PG for some rude humor and language

Dodgeball: A True Underdog Story   INTIMIDATION/PHYSICAL

Peter LeFleur (Vince Vaughn) owns a rundown gym where several oddballs congregate. White Goodman (Ben Stiller) owns a competitor, GloboGym and wants to wipe out the competition. Peter falls on hard times and he needs money to stave off foreclosure. He and his team enter a Dodgeball tournament to raise funds.

The scene opens on an educational film discussing the history and rules of the game of dodgeball. Patches O'Houlihan (Hank Azaria) enters to give strategies on winning the game. "But remember, dodgeball is a sport of violence, exclusion, and degradation. So, when you're picking players in gym class, remember to pick the bigger, stronger kids for your team. That way, you can all gang up on the weaker ones." The scene ends as Patches reviews the five D's of dodgeball.

> *Dodgeball: A True Underdog Story* (20th Century Fox, 2004), written and directed by Rawson Marshall Thurber
> **Elapsed Time:** This scene begins at 21:57 and ends at 24:27
> **Rating:** Rated PG-13 for rude and sexual humor, and language

Drillbit Taylor   PHYSICAL/BYSTANDER

Wade (Nate Hartley) and his friends fall on the bad side of Filkins, the high school bully. As a last resort, they hire a bodyguard, Drillbit Taylor (Owen Wilson) to protect them.

Wade (Nate Hartley) has just returned from school when his stepfather, Jim (Ian Roberts), notices Wade has a black eye. Wade explains "I was protecting this one kid in my school from a bunch of bullies and one of them punched me." "What? Why would you protect the kid from a bully?" Wade responds, "So he doesn't get beat up." Dad responds, "Then you're interfering with the natural order." He continues, "When I was a kid, I was kind of a bully. But, it's not a bad thing. There was this kid. I don't know what it was. Maybe it was his stupid face. But he'd just really get under my skin. So I pushed him around a little bit, called him some hurtful names, and I honestly think, if I met him today, he'd thank me for it. I prepared him for the harshness of the real world."

> ***Drillbit Taylor*** (20th Century Fox, 2004), written and directed by Rawson Marshall Thurber
> **Elapsed Time:** This scene begins at 45:31 and ends at 46:30
> **Rating:** Rated PG-13 for rude and sexual humor, and language

Drillbit Taylor   PHYSICAL/BYSTANDER
Wade (Nate Hartley) and his friends fall on the bad side of Filkins, the high school bully. As a last resort, they hire a bodyguard, Drillbit Taylor (Owen Wilson) to protect them.

It's the first day of high school and best friends, Wade (Nate Hartley) and Ryan (Troy Gentile), have accidentally worn identical shirts. They stand outside the school bus anticipating the year. As they are locating their lockers, they hear a young man's screams for help. Turning, they notice the boy being carried down the hall by his underwear by two older students, identified as Filkins (Alex Frost) and Ronnie (Josh Peck). The older students stuff the boy into a locker despite his screams "That's not for me. That's for my books! I am not a book!" Wade argues, "This is bad." Ryan counters, "No, this is good. At least we know we're not the biggest dorks in school." Wade questions whether they should intervene. Ryan argues "It's survival of the fittest." Wade feels he must say something, but Ryan urges him not to, "Say something? It's hilarious. The kid fits in the locker." Before intervening, Wade acknowledges, "This is the dumbest thing I've ever done." When the bullies realize Wade and Ryan are matching, they call them on it. The boy escapes from the locker and screams as he runs away "Everybody run! It's not safe here!" Filkins calls Wade and Ryan bitches who want to the wear the same shirt. They stuff Wade and Ryan into one shirt and threaten "You better keep that shit on, 'cause if I see you trying to take it off, you're dead. And you know what happens if one of you dies? Both of you dies, 'cause you're Siamese queers, bitches!" Wade and Ryan enter the classroom to the laughing scorn of their peers. Their teacher (Leslie Mann) mentions "That's very cute. You look like those Velcro monkeys who hug each other."

> ***Drillbit Taylor*** (20th Century Fox, 2004), written and directed by Rawson Marshall Thurber
> **Elapsed Time:** This scene begins at 7:32 and ends at 10:01
> **Rating:** Rated PG-13 for rude and sexual humor, and language

Drillbit Taylor   **PHYSICAL/INTIMIDATION**
Wade (Nate Hartley) and his friends fall on the bad side of Filkins, the high school bully. As a last resort, they hire a bodyguard, Drillbit Taylor (Owen Wilson) to protect them.

Because of their intervention Emmitt (David Dorfman) wants to hang with Wade and Ryan. As they walk down the hall, Filkins and Ronnie confront them. Ronnie states, "The Siamese queers had a baby." Filkins ponders, "I guess that makes them triplets, now doesn't it?" Emmitt retorts, "Well, actually, we still wouldn't be triplets, see. You see, they'd be my parents and I'd be the baby." Filkins interrupts, "Don't get smart with me. I said you're triplets and I think you guys need to get into his shirt [Emmitt is wearing the identical shirt that Wade and Ryan were wearing the previous day] and be triplets." Ryan queries, "Look, do you really have to do this crap, guys?" Pushing the trio back against the lockers, Filkins adds "Yeah. We have to do this shit because it's hilarious. This school is boring. Watching you freak out amuses me. And, yeah, it's just the second day of school. So guess what? It's gonna keep coming and coming and coming!" He grabs Wade by the throat and flicks his forehead. A montage ensues showing Filkins and Ronnie tormenting the young boys.

> ***Drillbit Taylor*** (20th Century Fox, 2004), written and directed by Rawson Marshall Thurber
> **Elapsed Time:** This scene begins at 10:47 and ends at 14:37
> **Rating:** Rated PG-13 for rude and sexual humor, and language

Drumline   **HAZING**
A superstar in his high school's marching band, Devon Miles (Nick Cannon) must learn the discipline to master the percussion cadence of his new university's band.

The new members of the band are required to perform various calesthenic drills by their squad leader including running up the bleachers while carrying their drums above their heads. A leader shouts "You can't wear my colors running like that!" A larger recruit carrying a French horn is insulted, "Let's go, Uncle Ben! I bet your country ass would run faster if I had one of your grandmama's hot butter biscuits." "I guess it ain't white boy day!" is directed towards a white male carrying his tuba. The team must do wall squats while they practice cadances even in the pouring rain. Sean (Leonard Roberts), the squad leader, singles out Jayson Flore (GQ) as a "crab." Jayson responds to his name "AKA, Affirmative Action [he is a white male attempting to join an HBCU band], brilliantly named by big brother Iron Man yesterday." Jayson cracks a joke and the other recruits laugh and are chided "Now you done messed up the cadence. Take it from the top!" The recruits groan.

> *Drumline* (Fox 2000 Pictures, 2002), written by Tina Gordon Chism and directed by Charles Stone III
> **Elapsed Time:** This scene begins at 17:11 and ends at 18:26
> **Rating:** Rated PG-13 for innuendo and language

Ella Enchanted VERBAL/HARASSMENT
Ella of Frell (Anne Hathaway) has been cursed by her fairy godmother, Lucinda, with a spell of obedience; she must obey every command, no matter how wicked. She goes on a quest to find Lucinda and along the way she unearths an evil plot to overthrow Prince Charmont's kingdom.

Ella's evil stepsisters learn Ella's secret—she must obey everything they say—even freeze in midair. They make her steal items in broad daylight, which gets her arrested. They even convince Ella to sabotage her relationship with her best friend, Arieda (Paraminder Nagra), by commanding Ella to state she "could never be friends with an Ayorithian" (Arieda's ethnic group). The scene ends when Ella closes the door on Arieda.

> *Ella Enchanted* (Miramax Films, 2004), written by Laurie Craig & Karen McCullah and directed by Tommy O'Haver
> **Elapsed Time:** This scene begins at 20:03 and ends at 24:36
> **Rating:** Rated PG for some crude humor and language

Fat Boy Chronicles, The INTIMIDATION/VERBAL
Ostracized by his peers as the "fat guy," Jimmy (Christopher Rivera) begins a plan to raise his popularity index by beginning a regimen to lose weight.

Jimmy Winterpock (Christopher Rivera) is changing in the locker room following gym class when Robb (Cole Carson) begins to call him "stupid" claiming "Don't you know? This is our spot." Jimmy tries to leave but is blocked. "Robb continues to berate him. "Hey cutie. Is this your locker room?" When another student approaches, Robb points at Jimmy's chest. "Look at that chest. It's bigger than Whitney's [Robb's girlfriend]. So, are you like a D-cup?" The coach interrupts and tells the boys to hurry up. After the coach leaves, Robb gathers the other students around, "Hey guys. I was thinking maybe we should change our mascot to the Big Round Blueberries." Robb and friends leave the locker room.

> ***The Fat Boy Chronicles*** (Tin Roof Films, 2010), written by Michael Buchanan & Diane Lang and directed by Jason Winn
> **Elapsed Time:** This scene begins at 11:20 and ends at 14:20
> **Rating:** NR

Final, The   REVENGE/HUMILIATION/DISCRIMINATION
Tired of being bullied by the jocks and popular kids, a group of outcasts plan a revenge party where they will show their tormentors what it's like to be preyed upon.

A group of teenagers are seated at a table in the cafeteria discussing their plot to take revenge on their bullies. Ravi (Vincent Siolchan) remarks, "I mean, all the years of watching horror films, what can be better than to put it all to use?" Suddenly, someone from the popular kids' table throws an open carton of milk on the teens. Riggs laughs, "Dude, he's fucking coming over here, man." Bernard scoffs, "Go back to India, bitch." Bernard mimics an Indian grocer and the crowd laughs while Ravi returns to his table.

> ***The Final*** (Agora Entertainment, 2010), written by Jason Kabolati and directed by Joey Stewart
> **Elapsed Time:** This scene begins at 8:34 and ends at 9:54
> **Rating:** Rated R for sadistic violence and torture, language, sexual references, drug and alcohol use—all involving teens

Final, The   PHYSICAL/DISCRIMINATION
Tired of being bullied by the jocks and popular kids, a group of outcasts plan a revenge party where they will show their tormentors what it's like to be preyed upon.

Ravi (Vincent Silochan) is in the bathroom putting batteries in his camera when Bernard (Daniel Ross Owens) and Riggs (Preston Flagg) enter. Bernard questions, "What do we have here, son, huh? If it isn't the *Slumdog Millionaire*." Riggs forms a pistol with his hands and points it at Ravi. "What's up Bin Laden?" Ravi responds, "I'm Indian, not Arab." Before placing Ravi in a headlock, he takes Ravi's camera and suggests Ravi is "doing a little recon for his terrorist cell." Riggs slams Ravi's camera to the ground in a mock football play, "Cause

THE BIG SHORT 89

I felt like it." Dane (Marc Donato) walks in looking for Ravi. Dane asks "Did you guys break his camera?" Riggs admits, "Yeah, I did. I busted it." Grabbing Dane by the throat, he continues, "The question is, what the fuck are you gonna do about it, huh?" Riggs challenges Dane to a fight, but Dane admits he can't beat Riggs. Riggs suggests, it's "'Cause you're a coward." Riggs argues, "You know why it is that I do what I do to you? Do you know? I do it because I know that you can't stop me?" Riggs tells Bernard "Let's leave these pussies." Dane puts a reassuring hand on Ravi and suggests "Soon."

> *The Final* (Agora Entertainment, 2010), written by Jason Kabolati and directed by Joey Stewart
> **Elapsed Time:** This scene begins at 13:13 and ends at 15:44
> **Rating:** Rated R for sadistic violence and torture, language, sexual references, drug and alcohol use—all involving teens

Final, The   REVENGE

Tired of being bullied by the jocks and popular kids, a group of outcasts plan a revenge party where they will show their tormentors what it's like to be preyed upon.

The bullied crew are sitting around a campfire. Andy (Travis Tedford) mentions, "I think I know what hell is. Hell is waking up every day believing that the suffering you're doing in life has meaning. That somehow, if you endure it, you gain valuable lessons. The truth is, sometimes you just suffer. There is no meaning." Jack (Eric Isenhower) picks up, "We're just pawns in a sick game of random chance. Chaos. Ravi (Vincent Silochan) adds, "My hell? Silence. The kind of silence that makes your ears ring." Dane interrupts, "Be glad for it. Mine's listening to my mom and dad fight day after day. Crashing plates. Screeching tires. Crying. I fucking hate the crying. I could use some silence. Andy queries, "Do you think we're going to hell?" Jack answers, "No. We've suffered enough." Dane continues, "We're doing God's work, as far as I'm concerned. Bring some justice into the world. Ravi, Emily, and Dane mediate on the peace they'll gain after their plan commences.

> *The Final* (Agora Entertainment, 2010), written by Jason Kabolati and directed by Joey Stewart
> **Elapsed Time:** This scene begins at 20:09 and ends at 22:10
> **Rating:** Rated R for sadistic violence and torture, language, sexual references, drug and alcohol use—all involving teens

Final, The   **REVENGE**

Tired of being bullied by the jocks and popular kids, a group of outcasts plan a revenge party where they will show their tormentors what it's like to be preyed upon.

The scene opens as Dane (Marc Donato) and his friends are attempting to waken their prisoners who question what is happening to them. Dane begins explaining, "There is actually a good explanation for all this....There's some good new and there's some bad news. The good news is, we don't plan to kill you. The bad news is, you will wish we had. Some of you will be spared, but you will all bear witness to the horror, just as you did in the hallways, just as you sat idly by as pain was inflicted upon us. What you fail to understand with reason, you will with wrath. Miles (Ryan Hayden) wonders, "Dude, what the fuck are you talking about?" Dane argues, "This is about what you are due. When we are done, you'll have a new perspective on life, and no one will ever look upon you the same again. You will forever be changed." After Miles is shot with a cattle gun, another student ponders, "Why us?" Dane answers, "You know, that's the same question we've been asking ourselves for years. Why us, always on the receiving end of your taunts, your laughter, and your childish cruelty? Now it's your turn to ask 'Why us'?" Answering the question "Who are you?," Dane says, "If you must know, we are the rejected, the humiliated; we are the outcasts. And tonight is our night, so relax. It's the only thing you can do." The scene ends when Dane tells Nadya about her boyfriend's infidelity.

> *The Final* (Agora Entertainment, 2010), written by Jason Kabolati and directed by Joey Stewart
> **Elapsed Time:** This scene begins at 33:40 and ends at 40:53
> **Rating:** Rated R for sadistic violence and torture, language, sexual references, drug and alcohol use—all involving teens

Final, The   **REVENGE**

Tired of being bullied by the jocks and popular kids, a group of outcasts plan a revenge party where they will show their tormentors what it's like to be preyed upon.

Dane (Marc Donato) asks the imprisoned bullies "Where did all this evil come from? What did I do to make someone hate me so much to go to these lengths? Think of this as the final, and there's only one question. What did I do to deserve this?" Brad cries aloud about his chains and asks, "What gives you the right to judge us, huh? What gives you the right to play God?" Dane laughs at Bradley's insinuation and responds, "God gave us the right. We gave him a chance to stop this. We gave him a chance to save all of you. But he chose to remain silent." Following this exchange, Bernard challenges, "Come on, fucker! I'm not scared of you. Bitch! Come on! You wanna fucking kill me? You fucking kill me, you motherfucker!" The masked reject stabs Bernard in the back with a sword and pours a chemical into his throat. The chemical renders Bernard unable to move, but he can still feel. Capitalizing on this, Emily sticks several needles into Bernard's neck. The scene ends as Kurtis escapes and Dane kills a member of his group.

> *The Final* (Agora Entertainment, 2010), written by Jason Kabolati and directed by Joey Stewart
> **Elapsed Time:** This scene begins at 42:27 and ends at 51:55
> **Rating:** Rated R for sadistic violence and torture, language, sexual references, drug and alcohol use—all involving teens

Final, The   REVENGE

Tired of being bullied by the jocks and popular kids, a group of outcasts plan a revenge party where they will show their tormentors what it's like to be preyed upon.

Heather (Julin) is restrained in a chair and Emily (Lindsay Seidel) is applying a chemical cream to her face that will burn her skin "dissolving it ever so slowly in the most painful way imaginable. And she will become outside what she is on the inside. Disgusting." Riggs (Preston Flagg) calls Dane (Marc Donato) a coward for masking himself. Dane argues, "I'm not hiding behind this mask. This is a reflection of what you turned me into. This is what I am on the inside. I am a monster that you created." After removing his mask, Dane states "You know, the irony of all this, you actually empowered me. I would have lived my life all alone in the shadows, unassuming. But you, you wouldn't allow me to do that. You had to torture me. You have nobody to blame for this but yourself."

> *The Final* (Agora Entertainment, 2010), written by Jason Kabolati and directed by Joey Stewart
> **Elapsed Time:** This scene begins at 54:15 and ends at 58:08
> **Rating:** Rated R for sadistic violence and torture, language, sexual references, drug and alcohol use—all involving teens

Final, The   **REVENGE**

Tired of being bullied by the jocks and popular kids, a group of outcasts plan a revenge party where they will show their tormentors what it's like to be preyed upon.

Bradley (Justin Arnold), in chains, pleads with Emily (Lindsay Seidel) to not hurt him. Bridget (Whitney Hoy) tells Emily (who is masked), "I know who you are." Emily and the others remove their masks. Bridget asks, "Are you doing this to get even with us? For how we treated you?" Emily sarcastically quips, "Can you think of a better reason?" Bridget apologizes, "I'm sorry for what we did. You didn't deserve it. Hurting us won't make you feel better. It won't fix anything. Please, just end it now. Let us all go." Emily responds, "Since you apologized, I won't hurt you. But for my generosity, you must do me a favor. I'm gonna need you to cut all of Bradley's fingers off." When Bridget argues that she can't do that, Emily leans close and says, "Either way, he gets what is due him. You do it, or we do it. It's the only way you can save yourself." Bridget cries, "I can't do this. I can't hurt anyone." Incredulous, Emily responds, "Sure you can. You hurt me. Without even blinking an eye." She continues, "That's a shame. I bet Bradley would cut your fingers off to save himself. [Turning to Bradley] "Save yourself from unimaginable pain by inflicting it." [Trying to goad Bradley] "Bradley, it's you or her. I know you'll need those fingers to play football. What would your life be without people cheering you on?"

> *The Final* (Agora Entertainment, 2010), written by Jason Kabolati and directed by Joey Stewart
> **Elapsed Time:** This scene begins at 58:47 and ends at 1:04:24
> **Rating:** Rated R for sadistic violence and torture, language, sexual references, drug and alcohol use—all involving teens

Final, The   **REVENGE/BYSTANDER**

Tired of being bullied by the jocks and popular kids, a group of outcasts plan a revenge party where they will show their tormentors what it's like to be preyed upon.

Dane (Marc Donato) and his friends have been torturing the popular kids who have bullied them. They are set to cut off the tongue of Riggs (Preston Flagg) when Kurtis (Jascha Washington) interrupts brandishing a gun. Kurtis tries to reason with Dane to stop what they are doing. Dane tells Kurtis that he is uninvited and should not be there. Kurtis says, "Fate brought me here to stop you." Kurtis has always been kind to Dane and company. Reflecting on this, Dane admits "You know, I wish there was more people like you. Then we wouldn't be here." The scene ends when Dane is shot by one of his own group.

> *The Final* (Agora Entertainment, 2010), written by Jason Kabolati and directed by Joey Stewart
> **Elapsed Time:** This scene begins at 1:25:17 and ends at 1:27:10
> **Rating:** Rated R for sadistic violence and torture, language, sexual references, drug and alcohol use—all involving teens

First Kid   PHYSICAL

Sam Simms (comedian Sinbad) is a secret service agent given the duty to protect the son of the president. Luke (Brock Pierce) just wants to be A normal kid and opens himself up to danger.

Luke Davenport (Brock Pierce) is the son of the U.S. president and goes to school under the watchful eye of Sam Simms (Sinbad), a Secret Service agent. Luke has drawn the ire and attention of Rob (Zachary Ty Bryan), the school bully. Rob continues to poke at Luke until Luke physically lashes out. Luke commanded Sam give him some space rather than being overprotective. Rob and the other student repeatedly push and insult Luke. Rob punches Luke in the face. Miss Lawrence (Fawn Reed), Luke's teacher yells at Sam for not protecting Luke. Sam defends saying Luke "The last thing he needs is support." Miss Lawrence retorts, "And what is it he needs?" Sam quickly responds, "He just got it."

> *First Kid* (Caravan Pictures, 1996), written by Tim Kelleher and directed by David M. Evans
> **Elapsed Time:** This scene begins at 27:03 and ends at 31:11
> **Rating:** Rated PG for some violence, language and brief partial nudity

Flirting   SOCIAL EXCLUSION/BIAS

At his boarding school, Danny (Noah Taylor) must fight against bullies and mean teachers. He falls in love with an African student named Thandiwe Adjewa (Thandie Newton) from a nearby school. Can their love survive the hostile environment?

The scene opens on footage of an old Tarzan movie and one of the students is mimicking Tarzan's primal yell. The students have all gathered in the dormitory hallway where it is announced that Danny (Noah Taylor) has received mail from his girlfriend. Several of the boys keep the letter from Danny. Bourke (Josh Picker) opens the letter and reads it aloud. In a voiceover, Danny narrates "People like to have someone to look down on. Makes them feel better about themselves. No one realized what a great community service I was performing by being the school dag [sic]. I didn't care."

> *Flirting* (Kennedy Miller Productions, 1991), written and directed by John Duigan
> **Elapsed Time:** This scene begins at 37:05 and ends at 38:21
> **Rating:** Rated R for scenes of teen sexuality

Geography Club PHYSICAL/HUMILIATION/BIAS

Students at a local high school go to great lengths to hide their sexual orientations—even joining the Geography Club.

Russell (Cameron Deane Stewart) has just entered the cafeteria where he sees his teammate, Jared (Dexter Darden) motioning for him to join him. Jared brings Russell into a janitor's closet where he and Kevin (Justin Deeley) have pinned down another student and have made him put on a sports bra. Kevin asks, "You see the sports bra? It's my sister's." Jared contends, "Look at him. He loves this." Kevin takes out a lipstick tube demanding Russell "Don't be a pussy, dude! Put it on him." Russell is reluctant. Jared says, "This is how we roll. Be a team player, bruh!" The trio push the unnamed student in his boxer shorts and bra out into the cafeteria amid the stunned and whispering students.

> *Geography Club* (Enumerated Pictures, 2013) written by Edmund Entin and directed by John Gary Entin
> **Elapsed Time:** This scene begins at 48:37 and ends at 50:03
> **Rating:** Rated PG-13 for thematic material involving sexuality and bullying, sexual content including references, language, and teen drinking

Girl Like Her, A PHYSICAL/CYBERBULLYING

This cinema verite film shows the harm caused to Jessica (Lexi Ainsworth) by her bully and tormentor, Avery (Hunter King).

This scene is a montage of several altercations between Jessica (Lexi Ainsworth) and her tormentor, Avery (Hunter King). Avery calls Jessica a "bitch" and bumps into her in the school hallway, She sends Jessica hurtful and obscene text messages then complains that Jess doesn't return her texts. Avery stops Jess from going to class. Avery mimics "Why didn't you respond to my texts? I thought we were friends. Why didn't you text me back? I was so nice to you." When Jess complains about being late for class, Avery states, "I don't give a fuck that you have to get to class!" Avery calls Jess "a disrespectful little cunt." Soon, Avery and her friends are found trashing Jessica's locker. Avery harasses Jessica constantly. She says, "Seriously, Jessica, if you disappeared, the world would be a better place. You're a fucking bitch! Why don't you just go kill yourself?" Speaking to her friends, Avery adds, "I have this funny feeling that she thinks that everything is just gonna get better from here on out. Just end it!" After an incident in the bathroom, Avery argues, "You think that I'm just gonna forget about you, gonna get bored with you? That's not the case, because I fucking hate you!" Later, Jessica's friend, Brian (Jimmy Bennett) finds Jessica crying in the hallway, "I just can't put up with it. I'm done. I can't do it anymore! I just don't know how much more I can take." Brian wants to show the secret videotapes of the harassment, but Jess cries, "It's embarrassing. I'm not showing this to anyone. It's not gonna get better, it's gonna get worse! It's never gonna end! I have no way out!" The scene ends with Jessica unconscious in the hospital after a suicide attempt.

A Girl Like Her (Radish Creative Group, 2015) written and directed by Amy S. Weber
Elapsed Time: This scene begins at 46:47 and ends at 53:31
Rating: Rated PG-13 for disturbing thematic material involving teens, and for language

Girl Like Her, A   PHYSICAL/INTIMIDATION
This cinema verite film shows the harm caused to Jessica (Lexi Ainsworth) by her bully and tormentor, Avery (Hunter King).

A documentary film crew has arrived at Brian's (Jimmy Bennett) house where he shows them the footage he and Jessica have been secretly recording Avery's (Hunter King) harassment. Brian tells the history of Avery's bullying, "It started slow, you know, it'd be like a bump here and there in the hallways. Like, nasty text messages or dirty looks. It just escalated and blew up. And Jess didn't feel very safe."

A Girl Like Her (Radish Creative Group, 2015) written and directed by Amy S. Weber
Elapsed Time: This scene begins at 42:13 and ends at 44:27
Rating: Rated PG-13 for disturbing thematic material involving teens, and for language

Going Greek   HAZING/HUMILIATION

Trying to stave off the loneliness of being a freshman, Jake Taylor (Dylan Bruno) opts to join a fraternity.

Pledgemaster Sully (Corey Pearson) is informing the pledges of the various tasks and duties they will be required to perform "that will constitute an important step on the path to brotherhood." Soon, the boys march into the library, pull down their underwear and perform "I'm a Little Teapot" naked in front of the library's patrons.

Going Greek (Little Fish Films, 2001) written and directed by Justin Zackham
Elapsed Time: This scene begins at 35:02 and ends at 35:59
Rating: Rated R for strong sexual content, language, crude humor, drug and alcohol use

Going Greek   HAZING

Trying to stave off the loneliness of being a freshman, Jake Taylor (Dylan Bruno) opts to join a fraternity.

The pledges are lined in formation and are marching on the lawn of the fraternity house. Big brothers Thompson (Simon Rex) and Ziegler (Oliver Hudson) are throwing eggs at the pledges. Ziegler hits a target and yells, "I love pledge invaders!"

Going Greek (Little Fish Films, 2001) written and directed by Justin Zackham
Elapsed Time: This scene begins at 36:48 and ends at 37:04
Rating: Rated R for strong sexual content, language, crude humor, drug and alcohol use

Going Greek   HAZING/HUMILIATION

Trying to stave off the loneliness of being a freshman, Jake Taylor (Dylan Bruno) opts to join a fraternity.

Gil (Dublin James) returns to his dorm room following a shower. He finds his roommate, Jake (Dylan Bruno), talking with Big Brother Davis (Chris Owen) about their pledge pins, which they've been told to always be wearing. Davis unrolls duct tape and threatens, "It's clobbering time." Moments later, two women are standing at the elevator. When the door opens, Gil is taped in a wheelchair. A large plastic dildo is taped to his forehead. A sign asks "What floor please?" Gil protests the tape being removed from his mouth. He motions to his sign. He uses the dildo to push the elevator's buttons.

Going Greek (Little Fish Films, 2001) written and directed by Justin Zackham
Elapsed Time: This scene begins at 41:11 and ends at 42:13
Rating: Rated R for strong sexual content, language, crude humor, drug and alcohol use

Hangman's Curse INTIMIDATION/PHYSICAL

An investigative team is called in to examine the reasons why kids who have reputations as bullies are going missing or turning up dead.

Blake (Edwin Hodge) and several friends are walking down their school's hallway discussing how several students have been injured. "I'm tired of this Abel Frye business. Alright? Kramer's still on the breathing machine. Anderson is critical. And now Jimmy." A female student mentions, "We know who's doing it." Another adds, "Yeah, I know, but they'll never believe us." Soon, two goth students are stopped by an athlete citing, "I ain't afraid of no ghost. What can a ghost do to me? Scare me out of cutting class? Tell Abel Frye his goose is cooked. And so is yours!" Ian (Jake Richardson) ponders, "What did I do?" The jock responds, "You're weird! That costs extra around here. Now you're buying me lunch, man." Taking money from Ian's pockets, "I'll keep the change."

Hangman's Curse (Namesake Entertainment, 2003) written by Kathy Mackel and directed by Rafal Zielinski
Elapsed Time: This scene begins at 9:51 and ends at 11:10
Rating: Rated PG-13 for elements of violence/terror and for brief drug material

Hearts in Atlantis PHYSICAL/INTIMIDATION

Bobby befriends an elderly man who has a mysterious power. Will Bobby learn too much?

Bobby (Anton Yelchin) is admiring a new Scwinn bicycle in a department store window. Later, he and his Carol Liz (Mika Boorem) are confronted by a group of boys led by Harry Doolin (Timothy Reifsnyder). Harry begins by calling Carol a "Gerber baby" and suggesting Bobby is her "little fairy." Bobby and Carol try to leave but are grabbed by Harry's companions. Liz complains, "This isn't funny!" Harry responds, "We think it's a riot, Gerber Baby." Bobby yells, "Lay off her!" Harry razzes, "Hey, the little guy's a hero." He begins pushing and poking Bobby" and challenging him to "Stop me, fairy. Be a man." Harry turns to Carol, "I asked how your tits were. I wanna feel for myself." Harry fondles Liz and complains, "She's just a Gerber Baby" and then suggests, "Let's beat this queer up." Just then, Ted (Anthony Hopkins) interrupts and calls Harry and friends the "unholy trio of St. Gabe's." Ted calls Harry over and tells him to apologize to Carol or he would unveil his dark secret of cross-dressing. Harry apologizes and the teens ride away.

> *Hearts in Atlantis* (Castle Rock Entertainment, 2001) written by Douglas Petrie & Theresa Rebeck and directed by Bronwen Hughes
> **Elapsed Time:** This scene begins at 1:08:17 and ends at 1:11:19
> **Rating:** Rated PG for mild language and some thematic elements

Holes   PHYSICAL

Boys at a juvenile detention camp are forced to dig holes to "build character." Might there be an ulterior motive behind the digging?

Dr. Pendanski (Tim Blake Nelson) is introducing Stanley (Shia LaBeouf) around the camp. He introduces him to his new mentor "Theodore" who prefers to be called the nickname "Armpit." Stanley asks Armpit where to fill up his canteen and Armpit violently places him in a headlock. Another juvenile asks Armpit why he's so mean. "Armpit defends, "Man, I ain't mean. I'm his mentor. Ain't that what I'm supposed to do?" Later, at dinner, when Stanley sits down to eat, X-ray (Brenden Jefferson) takes Stanley's bread.

> *Holes* (Walt Disney Pictures, 2003) written by Louis Sachar and directed by Andrew Davis
> **Elapsed Time:** This scene begins at 10:07 and ends at 14:07
> **Rating:** Rated PG for violence, mild language and some thematic elements

Hot Chick, The — HUMILIATION

An enchanted pair of earrings causes Jessica (Rachel McAdams) to switch bodies with a 30-year-old loser (played by Rob Schneider).

Jessica (Rachel McAdams) is the captain of the cheerleading squad and the squad is performing before a basketball game. Jessica invites Hildenberg (Megan Kuhlmann) to perform, but has required her to wear the uniform of the opposing team suggesting the theme is "unity...for all cheerleaders." Hildenberg performs to the jeers and boos of the audience who are throwing toilet paper rolls at her. Someone also hits Hildenberg with a toilet seat.

> *Hot Chick, the* (Touchstone Pictures, 2002) written by Tom Brady & Rob Schneider and directed by Tom Brady
> **Elapsed Time:** This scene begins at 2:19 and ends at 3:08
> **Rating:** Rated PG-13 on appeal for crude and sexual humor, language and drug references

How to Eat Fried Worms — PHYSICAL

The school bully dares his latest victim to eat a thermos of slithering worms. When Billy accepts the dare, the school's balance of power is upset.

Sitting on the picnic table at school, Billy (Luke Benward) and is approached by Adam (Austin Rogers). Adam shares his admiration for Billy for earlier throwing a worm into the face of Joe Guire. "I thought for sure he was gonna smash you with the death ring. Adam explains that if Joe punches with the death ring, "you die, but you don't die now. You die in eighth grade, so nobody can prove it." Adam worried that because Joe punched him, he was going to die in the 8th grade. Billy asked why Joe punched him. Adam answers, "Nothing. He just said I was annoying him for some reason." Adam reenacts how Joe punched him.

> *How to Eat Fried Worms* (Gran Via, 2006) written and directed by Bob Dolman
> **Elapsed Time:** This scene begins at 14:40 and ends at 16:22
> **Rating:** Rated PG for mild bullying and some crude humor

How to Eat Fried Worms — PHYSICAL

The school bully dares his latest victim to eat a thermos of slithering worms. When Billy accepts the dare, the school's balance of power is upset.

Billy (Luke Benward) is out running when he overhears a group of his classmates. They are searching for worms as Joe has challenged Billy to eat 10 worms. Adam (Austin Rogers) wonders aloud if eating worms is tantamount to eating chicken. Joe (Adam Hicks) picks up a worm and makes Adam eat it. Adam vomits and Billy runs away in terrific disgust. Later that night, Billy dreams about getting punched by Joe's death ring.

> *How to Eat Fried Worms* (Gran Via, 2006) written and directed by Bob Dolman
> **Elapsed Time:** This scene begins at 26:45 and ends at 28:39
> **Rating:** Rated PG for mild bullying and some crude humor

How to Eat Fried Worms　　　　　　　　　　**PHYSICAL/HUMILIATION**
The school bully dares his latest victim to eat a thermos of slithering worms. When Billy accepts the dare, the school's balance of power is upset.

As Billy opens his thermos at lunch, he is shocked to find that someone has filled it with earthworms. A student at a nearby table says, "Have a nice lunch." When the worms fall out, Bradley (Phillip Bolden) cheers and laughs. Joe mocks that Billy eats worms. Billy responds, "I eat them all the time. You want to try one?" Billy tosses one, but it lands on Joe's face. When Mr. Boilerhead enters the cafeteria, he quelches the ruckus and makes all the kids return to their seats. The scene ends as a student near Joe says, "He's gonna get it."

> *How to Eat Fried Worms* (Gran Via, 2006) written and directed by Bob Dolman
> **Elapsed Time:** This scene begins at 8:55 and ends at 11:02
> **Rating:** Rated PG for mild bullying and some crude humor

Invisible, The　　　　　　　　　　　　　　　　　　**PHYSICAL**
After being attacked, a teenager has been rendered invisible.

Annie (Margarita Levieva) is accosting Pete (Chris Marquette) accusing him of watching her by the lockers. Pete swears he was not involved. When he tries to run, Annie's goons capture him. Annie attempts to break Pete's hand.

> *The Invisible* (Hollywood Pictures, 2007) written by Mick Davis & Christine Roum and directed by David S. Goyer
> **Elapsed Time:** This scene begins at 22:54 and ends at 23:36
> **Rating:** Rated PG-13 for violence, criminality, sensuality and language—all involving teens

Invisible, The   PHYSICAL
After being attacked, a teenager has been rendered invisible.

Pete (Chris Marquette) is being beaten up and robbed in the school bathroom. When it's revealed that he doesn't have any money on him, Annie (Margarita Levieva) threatens him with a switchblade. She nicks his hand with it and she tells him, "Don't be such a baby. It's just a scratch." Leaving the bathroom, one of Annie's cronies adds, "See you soon."

> ***The Invisible*** (Hollywood Pictures, 2007)) written by Mick Davis & Christine Roum and directed by David S. Goyer
> **Elapsed Time:** This scene begins at 6:24 and ends at 7:26
> **Rating:** Rated PG-13 for violence, criminality, sensuality and language—all involving teens

Joe Somebody   PHYSICAL/INTIMIDATION
Sick of being bullied at work, Joe (Tim Allen) stands up to his workplace bully.

Joe (Tim Allen) and his daughter Natalie (Hayden Panettiere) are searching for a parking spot. As the gate opens, a random driver speeds past them. Joe cries out, "Hey, watch it, ass...guy!" As they are pulling into an open spot, the same driver careens into that spot. Natalie yells, "That guy's an asswipe...I meant an ass guy!" Joe recognizes him as Mark McKinney (Patrick Warburton) "a seven year employee" but wonders why he is parking in the 10-year employee lot. Joe confronts Mark regarding his improper parking. He argues, "Joe, I think walking from the west lot is probably better than getting your ass kicked in front of your little girl." Joe queries, "Are you like threatening to hit me?" Mark says, "I tell you what, Joe. I'm gonna give you to five to get back in your car." When Joe continues to refuse, Mark slaps him across the face.

> ***Joe Somebody*** (Fox Pictures, 2000, 2001) written by John Scott Shepherd and directed by John Pasquin
> **Elapsed Time:** This scene begins at 9:45 and ends at 12:22
> **Rating:** Rated PG for language, thematic elements and some mild violence

Just One of the Guys   PHYSICAL/INTIMIDATION
To win a coveted journalism contest, Terri (Joyce Hauser) becomes Terry and infiltrates the boy culture at a nearby high school.

Showing off his strength and athleticism, Greg (William Zabka) disrupts a table of outcasts/lunch by lifting their table while they eat. When that fails to get a rise out of them, he lifts their bench until several fall off.

Just One of the Guys (Columbia Pictures, 1985) written by Dennis Feldman & Jeff Franklin and directed by Lisa Gottlieb
Elapsed Time: This scene begins at 23:13 and ends at 23:45
Rating: Rated PG-13

Just One of the Guys   **PHYSICAL/INTIMIDATION**
To win a coveted journalism contest, Terri (Joyce Hauser) becomes Terry and infiltrates the boy culture at a nearby high school.

Terry (Joyce Hyser) enters the locker room for her/his first gym period. She/he notices several boys wearing nothing but jock straps. As s/he searches for a locker, someone screams out "Early shower squad—get the new kid!" Terry fears as it is her/his first day. She/he is relieved when another boy is chosen and carried off.

Just One of the Guys (Columbia Pictures, 1985) written by Dennis Feldman & Jeff Franklin and directed by Lisa Gottlieb
Elapsed Time: This scene begins at 23:25 and ends at 26:24
Rating: Rated PG-13

Just One of the Guys   **PHYSICAL/INTIMIDATION**
To win a coveted journalism contest, Terri (Joyce Hauser) becomes Terry and infiltrates the boy culture at a nearby high school.

It's Terry's first day at school in her new identity as a boy and as she approaches the doors, she notices Greg (William Zabka) demonstrating weight lifting strategies to his friends. Greg tells them "Once you're into power-blitzing, doing super sets is like jerking off. The key is to work out every possible minute. Like say you don't have any weights. You use freshmen." He demonstrates on a passing freshman. Terry uncomfortably laughs along until Greg wonders why he is there. Terry admits, "I'm new here." Greg remarks, "Just what we need—another pussy." Terry insults Greg and he continues his strength demonstration: "Another good exercise for upper body strength—the pussy toss for distance." Greg tosses Terry into the bushes.

> *Just One of the Guys* (Columbia Pictures, 1985)) written by Dennis Feldman & Jeff Franklin and directed by Lisa Gottlieb
> **Elapsed Time:** This scene begins at 17:46 and ends at 20:05
> **Rating:** Rated PG-13

Karate Kid, The PHYSICAL/BYSTANDER
Transplanted in California, Daniel LaRusso (Ralph Macchio) from New Jersey befriends the ex-girlfriend of a top martial arts champion.

Ali (Elisabeth Shue) and Daniel (Ralph Macchio) are playing on the beach when Johnny (William Zabka) and his friends approach on their motorcycles. Johnny and Ali recently broke up, and Johnny sees Daniel as a rival for her attention. Johnny harasses Ali and Daniel attempts to stand in for her, but Johnny beats him up and leaves him lying in the sand.

> *The Karate Kid* (Columbia Pictures, 1985) written by Robert Mark Kamen and directed by John G. Avildsen
> **Elapsed Time:** This scene begins at 11:20 and ends at 14:20
> **Rating:** Rated PG-13

Karate Kid, The PHYSICAL
Transplanted in California, Daniel LaRusso (Ralph Macchio) from New Jersey befriends the ex-girlfriend of a top martial arts champion.

Daniel (Ralph Macchio) is riding his bike alone at night. He notices Johnny and friends riding their motorcycles towards him. The boys begin to taunt: "Looking for a shortcut back to Newark, Daniel?" Johnny adds, "No, he wants to learn karate. Here's your first lesson: How to take a fall. Don't think about the pain." They push Daniel and cause him to fall down a nearby hill.

> *The Karate Kid* (Columbia Pictures, 1985) written by Robert Mark Kamen and directed by John G. Avildsen
> **Elapsed Time:** This scene begins at 25:19 and ends at 26:08
> **Rating:** Rated PG-13

Karate Kid II, The INTIMIDATION/BYSTANDER

Daniel LaRusso (Ralph Macchio) from New Jersey has beaten his rival at a karate competition. His teacher, Mr. Miyagi (Pat Morita) soon learns that he must return to Japan to settle some family business. Daniel accompanies him to Okinawa only to learn that the "business" is settling a rivalry with an old friend-turned-enemy.

The sequel picks up where the original ended. In this scene, Johnny (William Zabka) is being harassed by his coach, Mr. Kreese (Martin Kove), for losing the karate match to Daniel. Kreese tells Johnny "Second place is no place! You're off the team!" Johnny complains "I did my best!" Kreese responds, "You're nothing! You lost. You're a loser!" Mr. Miyagi (Pat Morita) intervenes. Kreese attempts to fight Miyagi, but is outsmarted. Acknowledging that he could have killed Kreese, Miyagi states, "For person with no forgiveness in heart, living is even worse punishment."

> *The Karate Kid II* (Columbia Pictures, 1986) written by Robert Mark Kamen and directed by John G. Avildsen
> **Elapsed Time:** This scene begins at 6:20 and ends at 9:20
> **Rating:** Rated PG-13

Killer Klowns from Outer Space INTIMIDATION/REVENGE
An appropriately named film.

An unnamed clown approaches a biker gang outside a bar. He is riding a motorized tricycle. Immediately, several of the bikers laugh and make fun of the little clown. Soon, a biker approaches and asks if he can ride the clown's bike. The clown refuses. The biker then asks to beep the horn. When the clown assents, the biker picks up the bike and smashes it to the ground. Another bikers whispers, "Should've let the man ride his bike." The biker sarcastically apologizes, "I'm sorry. I seemed to have broken your bike." The clown frowns and whines before jumping out of sight. He returns wearing boxing gloves and tells the biker "Put up your dukes." The biker asks, "What are you gonna do, knock my block off?" The clown responds with an uppercut, which decapitates the biker. The other bikers scramble and flee.

> *Killer Klowns from Outer Space* (Sarlui/Diamant, 1988) written by Charles Chiodo & Stephen Chiodo and directed by Stephen Chiodo
> **Elapsed Time:** This scene begins at 30:58 and ends at 32:42
> **Rating:** Rated PG-13

Let Me In   PHYSICAL/REVENGE

Owen gets bullied at school. That is, until he is befriended by Abby, who is a vampire hiding in secrecy.

Owen (Kodi Smit-McPhee) and Abby (Chloe Grace Moretz) are on the playground talking. Abby notes the bandage on Owen's face to whit Owen states, "Just some kids from school." Abby interrupts Owen to tell him, "You have to hit back. You have to hit back hard." Owen denies, "I can't. There's three of them." Abby continues to advise, "Then you hit back even harder. Hit them harder than you dare and then they'll stop." Owen queries, "What if they hit me back?" Abby offers her help if Owen's attempts don't work. "I'm a lot stronger than you think I am."

> *Let Me In* (Overture Films, 2010) written by Matt Reeves & John Ajvide Lindqvist and directed by Matt Reeves
> **Elapsed Time:** This scene begins at 39:03 and ends at 41:25
> **Rating:** Rated R for strong bloody horror violence, language and a brief sexual situation

Let Me In   PHYSICAL/AGGRESSION

Owen gets bullied at school. That is, until he is befriended by Abby, who is a vampire hiding in secrecy.

Owen (Kodi Smit-McPhee) hears loud banging outside the bathroom stall he's using. When he comes out Kenny (Dylan Minette) asks him to produce a drawing Owen was making earlier in class. Owen refuses and Kenny begins whipping Owen with a metal baton. Kenny swats Owen across the face. Donald (Nicolai Dorian), one of Kenny's friends, questions the wisdom of hitting Owen across the face. Kenny approaches Owen and grabs him by the hair and threatens, "It's OK. She's not going to tell her mom on us, is she? She fell down on the playground, that's all. Right? Right? Say it, little girl!" Later, with his mom, Owen tells her, "I fell down on the playground." Mom soothes, "You have to be more careful, okay, honey? I hate to see my baby get hurt."

> *Let Me In* (Overture Films, 2010) written by Matt Reeves & John Ajvide Lindqvist and directed by Matt Reeves
> **Elapsed Time:** This scene begins at 36:49 and ends at 38:55
> **Rating:** Rated R for strong bloody horror violence, language and a brief sexual situation

Let Me In PHYSICAL/INTIMIDATION/AGGRESSION

Owen gets bullied at school. That is, until he is befriended by Abby, who is a vampire hiding in secrecy.

Owen (Kodi Smit McPhee) is in the locker room getting his bookbag when Kenny (Dylan Minnette) calls him a liitle girl. Owen tries to escape him, but is blocked by Kenny's friends. Kenny repeatedly snaps his towel in Owen's face. Kenny suggests, "That's why he won't go swimming. He doesn't want everyone to see what a little fucking girl he is." When Owen tries to run away again, the boys pin him down while Kenny gives Owen a wedgie. Owen repeatedly yells for the boys to stop, but they only stop when they see that Owen has "pissed himself." One of the boys kicks Owen and shouts "Jesus Christ, fucking freak!" The boys depart the locker room cheering that "Owen pissed himself."

> *Let Me In* (Overture Films, 2010) written by Matt Reeves & John Ajvide Lindqvist and directed by Matt Reeves
> **Elapsed Time:** This scene begins at 15:58 and ends at 17:21
> **Rating:** Rated R for strong bloody horror violence, language and a brief sexual situation

Little Rascals, The INTIMIDATION

Against the rules of the "He Man Woman Haters' Club, Alfalfa wants to woo Darla.

Butch (Sam Saletta) and Woim (Blake Jeremy Collins) are test driving their stock car and happen upon Alfalfa (Bug Hall) as he walks down the street. Butch asks, "When's the last time we beat you up?" Alfalfa tries to jog his memory, "Yesterday." Butch yells, "You're due!" Alfalfa runs away and Butch and Woim chase him until they run through an auto painting shop and are spray painted blue.

> *The Little Rascals* (Universal Pictures, 1994) written by Paul Guay, Stephen Mazur, & Penelope Spheeris and directed by Penelope Spheeris
> **Elapsed Time:** This scene begins at 11:10 and ends at 12:40
> **Rating:** Rated PG for some rude dialogue

Lord of the Flies, The INTIMIDATION/PHYSICAL

The classic tale by Ian Fleming is adapted for the screen. A shipload of boys are stranded on a remote island when their ship crashes killing all of the adult chaperones. The boys divide into two factions.

THE BIG SHORT   107

The boys have separated into two factions. Ralph (Balthazar Getty) is attempting to call an assembly when Jack (Chris Furrh) asks "Why don't you just fuck off?" Jack and Ralph begin fighting. Piggy (Danuel Pipoly) blows the conch shell to stop the fight. He begins to speak about the potential for the boys to be lost on the island for years to come. As he is speaking, the boys taunt him and call him "Fat ass." Ralph notices that high above, one of the boys pushes a boulder off a cliff and it hits Piggy across the head and kills him.

> *The Lord of the Flies* (Castle Rock Entertainment, 1990) written by Jay Presson Allen and directed by Harry Hook
> **Elapsed Time:** This scene begins at 14:20 and ends at 17:05
> **Rating:** Rated R

Love Don't Cost a Thing   PHYSICAL/SOCIAL EXCLUSION
An urban retelling of 1980s hit Can't Buy Me Love.

Alvin (Nick Cannon) and his friends desire to be cool enough to be able to walk down the popular kids' hallway. They realize they do not have the social capital to do so because they are "invisible" to the popular crowd. Kenneth (Kal Penn) states, "in that community, we're immigrants without green cards." Fed up with being an outcast, Walter (Kenan Thompson) decides to walk down the hallway; he is immediately rebuffed. Walter tries to prove his coolness by revealing the label of his jeans. Ted (Al Thompson) pushes him against a locker and asks, "Is that the gay surrender? You a homo thug?" He threatens Walter with physical violence. The scene ends as Al and friends carry Walter away.

> *Love Don't Cost a Thing* (Alcon Entertainment, 2003) written by Michael Swerdlick & Troy Byer and directed by Troy Byer
> **Elapsed Time:** This scene begins at 9:39 and ends at 11:33
> **Rating:** Rated PG-13 for sexual content/humor

Lucas   INTIMIDATION/BYSTANDER
Smart but short, Lucas is promoted to high school. He faces trouble when the older, bigger boys want to show him the high school ropes.

Lucas (Corey Haim) and Maggie (Kerri Green) are at the concession stand at the movie theater with their friend, Ben (Ciro Poppiti) when Bruno (Tom

Hodges) begins chanting from afar "Luke, Luke, get that ball away and puke! Ben and Luke, I'm going to puke!" Ben tells Lucas not to allow Bruno to scare him away, but to "Tell him to eat shit." Ben stands up to Bruno and Cappie (Charlie Sheen) tries to calm the situation. Bruno continues, "This kid's mouthing off to me. I'm kidding around and this fat little marshmallow opens his mouth to me." Grabbing Lucas, Bruno goes on, "Be like Lucas. He's smart, not like you." Ben defends, "He's scared, not like me." Cappie continues to defend Lucas and company until Bruno leaves.

> *Lucas* (Twentieth Century Fox Film Corporation, 1986) written and directed by David Seltzer
>
> **Elapsed Time:** This scene begins at 25:08 and ends at 27:25
>
> **Rating:** Rated PG-13

Lucas   PHYSICAL/HUMILIATION

Smart but short, Lucas is promoted to high school. He faces trouble when the older, bigger boys want to show him the high school ropes.

After football practice, Lucas enters the shower and Bruno (Tom Hodges) begins making fun of Lucas' penis size. Lucas counters, "I don't get semi-erect around other males like some of you fellas do. You can tell the fags in a warm shower by who's got the longest dong." Pointing at Bruno, "Look, yours seems to be growing even now." The other team members take note and tease Bruno for getting a "hard-on." Spike (Jeremy Piven) charges, "Don't nobody bend over to pick up the soap." Members of the team grab Lucas and spread ointment on Lucas' genitals and lock him outside in a towel. Maggie (Kerri Green) arrives and attempts to talk to Lucas who is trying to find a place to calm the heat of the ointment. He sits atop a water fountain for relief.

> *Lucas* (Twentieth Century Fox Film Corporation, 1986) written and directed by David Seltzer
>
> **Elapsed Time:** This scene begins at 1:05:22 and ends at 1:08:15
>
> **Rating:** Rated PG-13

Martian Child   PHYSICAL/INTIMIDATION

Science-fiction writer, Gordon (John Cusack) takes in an imaginative youngster who believes he's from Mars.

As the scene opens, Dennis (Bobby Coleman) gets beaned in the face with a ball. He looks over and sees four older boys approaching him. He runs away and the narrator begins, "I suppose there's one in every group, one oddball who never fits in. That was me—David Gordon." Gordon (John Cusack) explains that he uses his writing to escape and "look at life from a safe distance."

> *Martian Child* (New Line Cinema, 2007) written by Seth Bass & Jonathan Tolins and directed by Menno Meyjes
> **Elapsed Time:** This scene begins at 0:43 and ends at 1:10
> **Rating:** Rated PG for thematic elements and mild language

Matilda   INTIMIDATION
Matilda (Mara Wilson) is a bit precocious and is misunderstood by her parents and school principal.

Mrs. Trunchbull (Pam Ferris) has taken the stage and calls for Bruce Bogtrotter (Jimmy Karz). She refers to Bruce as a "disgusting criminal" for eating her chocolate cake. Trunchbull makes Bruce eat an entire cake in front of the student body. The students' cheers and adulation empower Bruce to finish the feat. Trunchbull gives the cheering students 5 hours of after school detention.

> *Matilda* (TriStar Pictures, 1996) written by Nicholas Kazan and directed by Danny DevIto
> **Elapsed Time:** This scene begins at 37:13 and ends at 43:21
> **Rating:** Rated PG for elements of exaggerated meanness and ridicule, and for some mild language

Matilda   HUMILIATION/INTIMIDATION
Matilda (Mara Wilson) is a bit precocious and is misunderstood by her parents and school principal.

Mrs. Trunchbull (Pam Ferris) approaches Amanda Thripp (Jacqueline Steiger) for wearing pigtails in school. Trunchbull calls Amanda's mother a "twit." Trunchbull insists Amanda cut off her pigtails before school the next day. Trunchbull grabs Amanda by the pigtails and launches her into the field nearby in an epic hammer throw.

> *Matilda* (TriStar Pictures, 1996) written by Nicholas Kazan and directed by Danny DeVIto
> **Elapsed Time:** This scene begins at 26:05 and ends at 27:47
> **Rating:** Rated PG for elements of exaggerated meanness and ridicule, and for some mild language

Max Keeble's Big Move HUMILIATION/BYSTANDER
Max (Alex D. Linz) plots revenge against his bully when he learns that his family is moving. But what will happen if they don't move away?

Troy McGinty (Noel Fisher) stands on a bench in the school's hallway. He announces his latest target to bully by wearing the name on his t-shirt. He unzips his jacket to reveal "Freak with Robe." The scene shifts to the gym class of Robe (Josh Peck) running laps. Robe enters the locker room, but Troy grabs him saying, "Hello, freak." In the next scene, several students are watching, pointing, and laughing as Troy has stuffed Robe into a glass trophy case. Max (Alex Linz) releases him just before Robe vomits. The scene shifts to Dobbs (Orlando Brown) charging a male student to use the urinal. Troy busts in dragging Max and he asks Dobbs "How much for a swirlie?" Dobbs answers, "No charge" and opens a stall door.

> ***Max Keeble's Big Move*** (Walt Disney Pictures, 2001) written by Jonathan Bernstein, Mark Blackwell, & James Greer and directed by Tim Hill
> **Elapsed Time:** This scene begins at 28:01 and ends at 29:32
> **Rating:** Rated PG for some bullying and crude humor

Max Keeble's Big Move HUMILIATION/PHYSICAL
Max (Alex D. Linz) plots revenge against his bully when he learns that his family is moving. But what will happen if they don't move away?

Troy McGinty (Noel Fisher) has announced that Max Keebler will be his "First victim of the year—a big honor." In a voice-over, Max narrates his history with Troy: "You know the guy you hung out with when you were little, but as you got older you went in opposite directions? Well, Troy McGinty wasn't always a bully. I remember when he came to my fourth birthday. The theme was "MacGoogles the Frog." The scene cuts to a televised image of MacGoogles and a younger Troy crying "I don't like MacGoogles!" The other kids at the party call Troy a "scaredy cat" when he flinches when Max's dad enters dressed in a MacGoogles costume. Fast forward to Troy carrying Max down the hallway and outside to a mud puddle where he throws Max. Two other students excitedly take a picture before Troy dumps a load of sawdust on Max. Troy finishes by tossing Max in the dumpster.

> *Max Keeble's Big Move* (Walt Disney Pictures, 2001) written by Jonathan Bernstein, Mark Blackwell, & James Greer and directed by Tim Hill
> **Elapsed Time:** This scene begins at 12:28 and ends at 14:14
> **Rating:** Rated PG for some bullying and crude humor

Max Keeble's Big Move   **INTIMIDATION**

Max (Alex D. Linz) plots revenge against his bully when he learns that his family is moving. But what will happen if they don't move away?

Marley (Jordan Mahome) is dictating the school's history of bullying. He admits "Curtis Junior High has a long and fascinating history of colorful bullies." He describes, "In 1985, Tomato-face Callahan. He'd walk right up and shove a tomato in your face. 1991, Wedgie Jackson. He invented the world wide wedge. Which brings us to this year. Troy McGinty." The scene shifts to Troy, clad in all black, chains, and boots. Marley continues, "Word is, he's gonna pound on a different kid every day. And he's devised his own special way of letting the world know who he's coming after." Troy unzips his jacket to show Max Keeble's name and the growd gasps.

> *Max Keeble's Big Move* (Walt Disney Pictures, 2001) written by Jonathan Bernstein, Mark Blackwell, & James Greer and directed by Tim Hill
> **Elapsed Time:** This scene begins at 8:28 and ends at 9:14
> **Rating:** Rated PG for some bullying and crude humor

Mean Creek   **PHYSICAL/AGGRESSION**

Hoping to punish his bully, Sam (Rory Culkin) and his friends lead George (Josh Peck) into the woods.

George (Josh Peck) sets up his video camera to record himself playing basketball. Sam (Rory Culkin) sees the unattended camera and picks it up. George goes ballistic when he sees Sam, "Hey! What do you think you're doing? You're a punk, Sam! I ought to kill you! You fucking dickhead! I told you to never touch my camera! Didn't I? Fucker! You little wimp! Bitch! Pussy! I told you! I ought to fucking kill you! And I will kill you, you little punk, if

I ever catch you fucking with my camera again." George is beating on Sam throughout his tirade.

> *Mean Creek* (Whitewater Films, 2004) written and directed by Jacob Estes
> **Elapsed Time:** This scene begins at 1:46 and ends at 2:43
> **Rating:** Rated R for language, sexual references, teen drug and alcohol use

Mean Creek   PHYSICAL/INTIMIDATION
Hoping to punish his bully, Sam (Rory Culkin) and his friends lead George (Josh Peck) into the woods.

Marty (Scott Mechlowicz) is target shooting with his brother's gun. As he prepares to shoot, he remarks "Kiss my ass, Mr. Shaham. Kiss my ass, Mr. Estes. Kiss my ass, Ms. Johnson. Kiss my ass, Mr. Rosenthal." Exclaiming "Shit!" when he misses, Kile (Branden Williams), his brother, comes out to complain why Marty is not in school. "Fuck school!" Marty responds. When Marty argues that Kile is not his father, Kile grabs his ear and yells, "Yeah, you're right, I'm not Dad. Dad didn't yank as hard as I do. Kile takes his gun back charging, "Look, stupid. You ever take this without my permission again, I guarantee it, you'll be sorry." The scene concludes with Marty hitting a liquor bottle with a baseball bat and declaring, Kiss my ass, Kile."

> *Mean Creek* (Whitewater Films, 2004) written and directed by Jacob Estes
> **Elapsed Time:** This scene begins at 12:17 and ends at 14:06
> **Rating:** Rated R for language, sexual references, teen drug and alcohol use

Mean Girls   SOCIAL EXCLUSION
Homeschooled Cady (Lindsay Lohan) has grown up in Africa. She has a lot to learn about American high schools—particularly the power of the popular female clique.

Cady (Lindsay Lohan) narrates "Eating lunch with the Plastics was like leaving the actual world and entering 'Girl World.' And Girl World had a lot of rules." Gretchen (Lacey Chabert) begins the list of rules. After detailing the rules, Gretchen adds, "Now, if you break any of these rules, you can't sit with us at lunch. I mean, not just you. Like, any of us." Gretchen further explains rules about clothing styles and dating. "Ex-boyfriends are just off-limits to friends. I mean, that's just, like, the rules of feminism."

> *Mean Girls* (Paramount Pictures, 2004) written by Tina Fey and directed by Mark Waters
> **Elapsed Time:** This scene begins at 13:37 and ends at 15:20
> **Rating:** Rated PG-13 for sexual content, language and some teen partying

Meatballs   INTIMIDATION
Rookie and returning camp counselors balance hijinks and growing up with teens at a summer camp.

As the teens are arriving at the parking lot to load the busses for camp, camp counselor, Spazz, wanders over to the local K-Mart to get a milkshake. As he is exiting, he is accosted by several men, one of whom pours the milkshake over Spazz's head.

> *Meatballs* (Canadian Film Development Corporation, 1979) written by Len Blum & Daniel Goldberg and directed by Ivan Reitman
> **Elapsed Time:** This scene begins at and ends at
> **Rating:** Rated PG

My Bodyguard   INTIMIDATION
Wanting to escape the clutches of the school bully, Clifford (Chris Makepeace) hires some protective help from a tough kid.

Moody (Matt Dillon) enters the classroom to much fanfare. When the teacher asks him to find a seat, Moody looks at Clifford (Chris Makepeace) and declares "This sucker swiped it from me." Chris defends, "I was here first!" Moody returns, "Bullshit!" The teacher continues to take attendance. When she gets to Clifford's name, she asks for the correct pronunciation. He says it's "Peach." Moody announces, "I knew he was a fruit." Moody desires to be called "Big M;" Clifford remarks, "Is that 'B.M.' for short?" Sensing Moody's ire, Reissman (Tom Rielly) adds, "You've got nerve, even if you're not gonna live long." Moody tells Clifford, "You and me, we're gonna have a little talk after school." In a later class, Reissman tells Clifford, "You know that was so dumb what you said to Moody this morning. I never saw anybody put him down before. I hope you get away with it...Don't let him catch you in the halls alone, or on the stairs either. Or especially in the bathrooms. I never go to the bathroom here, if I can help it. They say one kid got thrown out a window last year. He's a vegetable now.

Another guy had his eye kicked out. Total gross-out." Clifford wonders if Moody was responsible for hurting the other kid. Reissman defends, "I'm not saying he did, and I'm not saying he didn't. But from my point of view, you're better off paying him protection money." Reissman explains how Moody takes kids lunch money, so he brings his lunch to school. "Now he claims he's gonna take my bus fare." Clifford suggests not allowing Moody to get away with it, but Reismman declares, "I know, but I'm kind of addicted to breathing."

> *My Bodyguard* (Twentieth Century Fox Film Corporation, 1980) written by Tina Fey and directed by Mark Waters
> **Elapsed Time:** This scene begins at 13:26 and ends at 17:21
> **Rating:** Rated PG

My Bodyguard   PHYSICAL/INTIMIDATION
Wanting to escape the clutches of the school bully, Clifford (Chris Makepeace) hires some protective help from a tough kid.

Clifford (Chris Makepeace) is walking down the hall after school when he is delivered by a couple young men to Moody in the boys' bathroom. Moody (Matt Dillon) is currently involved with harassing a different boy and demanding that boy to give him a dollar every day. Moody slings wet wads of toilet paper at Clifford's head. Moody scoops a cup of filth from the toilet and demands Clifford eat it. Clifford throws the contents in Moody's face and flees the bathroom.

> *My Bodyguard* (Twentieth Century Fox Film Corporation, 1980) written by Tina Fey and directed by Mark Waters
> **Elapsed Time:** This scene begins at 18:40 and ends at 22:23
> **Rating:** Rated PG

Napoleon Dynamite   PHYSICAL
Napoleon (John Heder) wants to help Pedro get elected student body president. He does so while dealing with his odd family.

Randy (Bracken Johnson) is holding another student by his neck and demanding the kid give him "50 cents to buy a pop." When the boy doesn't give him the money, Randy jerks his head repeatedly. Randy stops as the school bell rings. Napoleon (Jon Heder) wonders how the boy's neck feels and gives him a trinket saying, "Pedro offers you his protection." Later, Randy approaches the same student and tries to take his bike. A car with a decal on the side reading "Vote for Pedro" approaches and two very tough looking Latinos shake their heads and Randy runs away.

> *Napoleon Dynamite* (Fox Searchlight Pictures, 2004) written by written by Jared Hess & Jerusha Hess and directed by Jared Hess
> **Elapsed Time:** This scene begins at 1:01:33 and ends at 1:02:46
> **Rating:** Rated PG for thematic elements and language

Not Another Teen Movie   SOCIAL EXCLUSION/VERBAL
In this satirical take on high school movies, Janey (Chyler Leigh) is the girl in the ponytail with the glasses who becomes the love interest of the popular boys who accepts a bet.

Janey (Chyler Leigh) stands on a balcony at a party and jumps into the pool. When she gets out of the pool, Priscilla (Jaime Pressly) and her friends approach Janey and question her presence at the party. Priscilla argues, "Look, you may have lost those glasses and that ponytail thing you do, but to everyone that matters, you're still a loser." Priscilla pours a bottle of water on Janey and challenges her not to cry. Janey runs away crying.

> *Not Another Teen Movie* (Columbia Pictures Corporation, 2001) written by Mike Bender & Adam Jay Epstein and directed by Joel Gallen
> **Elapsed Time:** This scene begins at 43:21 and ends at 44:50
> **Rating:** Rated R for strong crude sexual content and humor, language and some drug content

Odd Girl Out   SOCIAL EXCLUSION
A young highschooler is ostracized by her former friends when she becomes a rival for a boy's attention.

A group of girls are seated in the cafeteria. Tiffany (Alicia Morton) is telling a story, "Her clothes were hideous. And I was looking at her hair style; it was horrible, and I was, like, 'Who does your hair, the gardener?'" Soon, Vanessa (Alexa PenaVega) approaches and tries to sit down but Nikki blocks her. "Oh, come on, Nik, I know you have an SUV for an ass, but just park it in one spot." Nikki deflects, "There's plenty of room over there." Tiffany calls Vanessa a "slut." The scene ends when Vanessa goes to another table.

Odd Girl Out (Jaffe/Braunstein Films, 2005) written by Richard Kletter and directed by Tom McLoughlin

Elapsed Time: This scene begins at 17:41 and ends at 19:10

Rating: Rated PG-13 for mature thematic issues and language

Odd Girl Out   SOCIAL EXCLUSION

A young highschooler is ostracized by her former friends when she becomes a rival for a boy's attention.

Vanessa (Alexa PenaVega) has been ostracized to the "losers' table" in the cafeteria. She has been befriended by Emily (Shari Perry) who tells her she missed the action in English class. Emily tells Vanessa, "You know why they keep dogging you? They do it because they know it gets to you. I call them the 'white tornadoes' because they destroy whatever's in their path." Soon, another female student brings over a laptop showing a meme of Vanessa eating and getting fatter while onlookers laugh. Later, Vanessa approaches Tony (Chad Biagini) at his locker and he shuns her.

Odd Girl Out (Jaffe/Braunstein Films, 2005) written by Richard Kletter and directed by Tom McLoughlin

Elapsed Time: This scene begins at 23:06 and ends at 25:45

Rating: Rated PG-13 for mature thematic issues and language

Odd Girl Out   CYBERBULLYING

A young highschooler is ostracized by her former friends when she becomes a rival for a boy's attention.

Vanessa (Alexa PenaVega) is working at her computer. She receives an instant message to follow a hyperlink. The link takes her to a website titled "Hating Vanessa" with an image of Vanessa with an inflated butt. The site's tagline asks, "Should a friend tell a friend when she's getting FAT?" Vanessa exits the site.

Odd Girl Out (Jaffe/Braunstein Films, 2005) written by Richard Kletter and directed by Tom McLoughlin

Elapsed Time: This scene begins at 30:02 and ends at 30:50

Rating: Rated PG-13 for mature thematic issues and language

THE BIG SHORT   117

Odd Life of Timothy Green, The   PHYSICAL

Timothy's newly adoptive parents must learn to protect Timothy at all costs. He is a "special" kid for sure and they must keep his secret while they try to figure out how to keep him alive.

Principal Morrison (Sharon Conley) has invited Timothy's parents, Cindy (Jennifer Garner) and Jim (Joel Edgerton) to her office following an incident. Timothy (CJ Adams) explains how he became an "art project." The scene shifts to a larger student rubbing food on Timothy's face when Joni (Odeya Rush) comes up the stairs. She places a cherry on top of Timothy's head and he smiles. Jim swings Timothy's chair around and tells him, "Timothy, this kind of thing happened to me when I was your age. And all I wanted was for my dad to have my back, and he didn't. So here's what we're going to do. You're going to tell me the names of the boys that did this to you. And I will handle it." Timothy whispers into Jim's ear. Jim next appears on his boss' doorstep; he is none too pleased that "Your kid ratted my boys out." Cindy turns to Timothy and says, "You can't let people treat you like this." Mr. Crudstaff (Ron Livingston) asks Jim "Are you really going to fight all his battles for him? You think that's wise?" Bobby Crudstaff (William Harrison) explains "We were just having fun. He didn't fight back. He didn't even cry. It wasn't any fun. The social worker, Evette Onat (Shohreh Aghdashloo), wonders why the Greens "took him back to the house of the boys who bullied him." Cindy answers, "He really, really wanted to go." Jim adds, "I thought it was time he learned to fight his own battles." The scene ends as Timothy jumps off the diving board at a pool party.

The Odd Life of Timothy Green (Monsterfoot Productions, 2012) written and directed by Peter Hedges
Elapsed Time: This scene begins at 34:57 and ends at 39:05
Rating: Rated PG for mild thematic elements and brief language

Perks of Being a Wallflower, The   PHYSICAL/BYSTANDER

Tells the tale of a group of friends as they navigate the last days of high school.

Brad (Johnny Simmons) and Patrick (Ezra Miller) have been having a secret relationship until Brad's dad caught them and had physically assaulted Brad. Charlie (Logan Lermon) learns about this and sees the bruises on Brad's face. Later, in the cafeteria, Patrick is walking and is tripped by a student. Patrick scolds Patrick for not speaking up for him. But Brad tries to maintain the secrecy of their relationship. Patrick threatens to "out" Brad, who responds, "I don't know what kinda sick shit you're trying to pull, but you better walk away right now." Brad calls Patrick a "faggot" and Patrick punches him in the face. Brad's friends begin beating Parick, but Charlie steps in and finishes the students. Charlie warns, "Touch my friends again and I'll blind you." Once he's released from the principal's office, Charlie runs into Sam (Emma Watson) who tells Charlie, "You saved my brother."

> *The Perks of Being a Wallflower* (Summit Entertainment, 2012) written and directed by Stephen Chbosky
> **Elapsed Time:** This scene begins at 1:09:30 and ends at 1:14:00
> **Rating:** Rated PG-13 on appeal for mature thematic material, drug and alcohol use, sexual content including references, and a fight—all involving teens

Perks of Being a Wallflower, The   **HAZING**
Tells the tale of a group of friends as they navigate the last days of high school.

In a voiceover, Charlie (Logan Lerman) narrates while he writes in his journal. He speaks of not wanting to be the kid who spent time in a mental hospital. He imagines what it will be like on his first day of high school. "As I enter the school for the first time, I will visualize what it will be like on the last day of my senior year. Unfortunately, I counted and that's 1, 385 days from now." A group of freshman students are being made to hop down the hall like toads. "Just 1,385 days." Charlie continues to describe how he had hoped to sit with his older sister, Candace (Nina Dobrev) at lunch. She rebuffs him, "Seniors only."

> *The Perks of Being a Wallflower* (Summit Entertainment, 2012) written and directed by Stephen Chbosky
> **Elapsed Time:** This scene begins at 1:55 and ends 3:21
> **Rating:** Rated PG-13 on appeal for mature thematic material, drug and alcohol use, sexual content including references, and a fight—all involving teens

Powder   **INTIMIDATION/HAZING**
Born under special circumstances, Powder has no skin pigmentation, but he has developed a set of special skills that make him a target for harassment.

Powder (Sean Patrick Flanery) is eating his lunch alone in the cafeteria. Soon, John (Bradford Tatum) and several other boys join him. John asks, "Why do you look like that? You look like some kind of vampire from outer space or something. They kick you out of cancer camp?" Powder ignores John, but John continues, "You got some kind of disease?" John begins to tease, "I don't like your eyes" and pulls Powder's tray away. John turns to the other students and asks, "What's a new guy gotta do the first day he gets here?" Another student chimes in, "He's gotta do the due." John adds, "New guy, first day, first meal. He's gotta wear his spoon." John tells Powder, "You've got two choices. You can either wear it on the end of your nose—or you can wear it the other way, which is up your ass. You choose." Powder rubs the spoon causing it to become magnetized and pulls all the other silverware in the cafeteria.

> *Powder* (Caravan Pictures, 1995) written and directed by Victor Salva
> **Elapsed Time:** This scene begins at 20:02 and ends 24:45
> **Rating:** Rated PG-13 for intense, sometimes frightening elements of theme, and for language

Powder   INTIMIDATION/PHYSICAL
Born under special circumstances, Powder has no skin pigmentation, but he has developed a set of special skills that make him a target for harassment.

Powder (Sean Patrick Flanery) enters the gymnasium at his school. He notices Skye (Reed Frerichs) cooling off in the shower. John (Bradford Tatum) queries, "Why don't you take a picture, man?" John alerts Skye to the "Peeping Tom faggot." Powder tries to leave and John takes his hat and challenges "You think you can take me, freak show, go for it." Powder is able to psychically read John's mind from a time when John's stepfather had a similar altercation with John. Powder reminiscing, "'I'd beat you to shit before you got this old hat back.' And then he beat you bloody that night when you tried." John cried out, "Hey, fuck you!" Powder continues, "You had marks so dark, you were embarrassed to suit up for gym." John responds, "I ought to kill you right now. I ought to slit your throat and spit down it while I'm doing it." Johnny drags Powder outside and strips him naked and kicks him into a mud puddle. John whispers in Powder's ear, "You really think you can be like us? Is that what you think, freak show?

> *Powder* (Caravan Pictures, 1995) written and directed by Victor Salva
> **Elapsed Time:** This scene begins at 1:27:45 and ends 1:33:45
> **Rating:** Rated PG-13 for intense, sometimes frightening elements of theme, and for language

Prom   HAZING/HUMILIATION

Ahh…Prom. The night of tuxedos and ball gowns representing a rite of passage for teens.

Nova (Aimee Teegarden) happens upon Lucas (Nolan Soltillo) and his friend in the hallway wearing hockey helmets. She queries and Lucas says, "Uh, varsity made us wear them…it's humiliating." Nova responds, "I think it's cute."

> **Prom** (Rickshaw Productions, 2011) written by Katie Wech and directed by Joe Nussbaum
> **Elapsed Time:** This scene begins at 22:42 and ends at 23:26
> **Rating:** Rated PG for mild language and a brief fight

Radio   HUMILIATION/DISCRIMINATION

Despite his special needs, Radio (Cuba Gooding, Jr.) helps the high school football coach.

Radio (Cuba Gooding, Jr.) is cleaning up in the coach's office when several other boys tell him that Coach Dalrymple needs help in the girls' locker room. Radio complies as not to disappoint. Radio goes into the locker room and several girls scream. Radio runs out whimpering, "Bad Radio. Bad Radio." Later, Radio refuses to tell on the boys who goaded him.

> **Radio** (Revolution Studios, 2003) written by Mike Rich and directed by Michael Tollin
> **Elapsed Time:** This scene begins at 1:11:12 and ends at 1:14:25
> **Rating:** Rated PG for mild language and thematic elements

Read It and Weep   SOCIAL EXCLUSION

Jamie's diary becomes a best seller.

Lindsay (Marquise C. Brown) and Jamie (Kay Panabaker) are handing out fliers in the hallway when Jamie notices "the populars" and their leader Sawyer (Allison Scagliotti). Sawyer and her "clone horrific cohort" tease Jamie about cheerleader tryouts. Writing about Sawyer in her manuscript, Jamie voices, "Risking life and limb, Iz knew she had to destroy Myrna [Sawyer] and her vicious clique before they crushed every girl's spirit."

> *Read It and Weep* (Just Singer Entertainment, 2006) written by Patrick J. Clifton & Beth Rigazio and directed by Paul Hoen
> **Elapsed Time:** This scene begins at 3:50 and ends at 5:20
> **Rating:** Rated TV-G

Return to Sleepaway Camp   PHYSICAL/HUMILIATION
At Camp Manabe, kids torment each other and soon things go awry.

When Alan (Michael Gibney) loudly complains about the food he was served, his fed-up counselor, Randy, grabs him by the neck and forcefully pushes his head down towards his plate while yelling, "Eat the fucking chicken, Alan!" Randy slams Alan to the ground and calls him a "pussy." Alan complains to Ronnie (Paul DeAngelo), "I'm trying, Ronnie, but everybody keeps picking on me 'cause I'm different." As Alan tries to leave the cafeteria, Bella (Shahida McIntosh) punches him in the chest "Because your face looks like my ass. Problem?" Alan dumps Bella's plate on her lap and departs.

> *Return to Sleepaway Camp* (Go2Sho, 2008)) written by and directed by Robert Hiltzik
> **Elapsed Time:** This scene begins at 6:35 and ends at 8:38
> **Rating:** Rated R for horror violence and gore, pervasive language, some sexual content and teen drug use

Return to Sleepaway Camp   HUMILIATION/INTIMIDATION
At Camp Manabe, kids torment each other and soon things go awry.

A group of boys are in their cabin. To pass the time, they are "lighting farts." Alan (Michael Gibney) enters the room and presumes the boys are laughing at him. He threatens and hurls insults at them. Alan creates a flamethrower with the lighter and hairspray and threatens the boys with it. Randy enters and pushes Alan away, asking "Are you out of your fucking mind?" Alan calls Randy a "big penis" and runs out. Randy promises "I'm gonna teach that little prick a lesson he won't forget!"

> *Return to Sleepaway Camp* (Go2Sho, 2008) written by and directed by Robert Hiltzik
> **Elapsed Time:** This scene begins at 1:56 and ends at 3:45
> **Rating:** Rated R for horror violence and gore, pervasive language, some sexual content and teen drug use

Rocky V   **PHYSICAL/REVENGE**

The fifth installment of the Rocky franchise finds Rocky training a young protégé.

Rocky, Jr. (Sage Stallone) and his friend, Jewel (Elisebeth Peters) have grown weary of their bullies and decide to stand up to them. Chickie (Kevin Connolly) threatens, "Two more steps, and I'm gonna pound your teeth out!" Rocky beats Chickie up. At the conclusion, Rocky offers, "If you wanna end it, let's end it now." The two shake hands and go their separate ways.

> ***Rocky V*** (United Artists, 1990) written by Sylvester Stallone and directed by John G. Avildsen
> **Elapsed Time:** This scene begins at 58:16 and ends at 59:22
> **Rating:** Rated PG-13

Rocky V   **PHYSICAL**

The fifth installment of the Rocky franchise finds Rocky training a young protégé.

Rocky (Sage Balboa) has been having trouble making friends at his new school. Several kids notice him as the son of Rocky Balboa, the champion boxer. They befriend him and all of a sudden turn on him, assault him, and steal his jacket. As the boys run away, Chickie (Kevin Connolly) yells, "Don't catch cold, rich boy!"

> ***Rocky V*** (United Artists, 1990) written by Sylvester Stallone and directed by John G. Avildsen
> **Elapsed Time:** This scene begins at 38:20 and ends at 39:06
> **Rating:** Rated PG-13

Rocky V   **PHYSICAL**

The fifth installment of the Rocky franchise finds Rocky training a young protégé.

Rocky (Sage Stallone) is walking down the street when Chickie (Kevin Connolly) and his pal accost him. Chickie asks, "Hey, rich boy, how much money you got in your pocket today?" The boys push Rocky into an alleyway where they beat him up and steal his money.

THE BIG SHORT   123

> *Rocky V* (United Artists, 1990) written by Sylvester Stallone and directed by John G. Avildsen
> **Elapsed Time:** This scene begins at 51:30 and ends at 51:52
> **Rating:** Rated PG-13

Rocky V   REVENGE

The fifth installment of the Rocky franchise finds Rocky training a young protégé.

Rocky Jr. (Sage Stallone) comes home with a bruise on his cheek and his father inquires "So why'd this kid smack your face for, huh?" Rocky responds, "It doesn't really matter, Dad." When his mother says she is going to go to the school, Rocky responds, "You'll make things worse if you go! Can't I do what I think is right?" Paulie (Burt Young) suggests "a baseball bat across the face" as the solution. Tommy (Tommy Gunn) reminisces about a kid who bothered him in school. He says his mother told him to "Pretend the guy's like a balloon. If you pop him hard, this guy's gonna go away." Adrian (Talia Shire) counters, "Tommy, we're trying to raise our son, so he can handle his problems with his mind, not his muscles. Rocky adds, "That's why I'm gonna get mangled." Rocky Jr. asks Rocky, Sr. (Sylvester Stallone) to teach him how to fight. Paulie mentions the baseball bat, again. Senior mentions, "Adrian, I don't think it would be so bad if I taught him how to throw a few deadly punches." Tommy shares how his father would physically abuse him and his mother. The scene ends as Rocky offers Tommy a place to stay for the night.

> *Rocky V* (United Artists, 1990) written by Sylvester Stallone and directed by John G. Avildsen
> **Elapsed Time:** This scene begins at 46:20 and ends at 49:15
> **Rating:** Rated PG-13

School Ties   VERBAL/DISCRIMINATION

In the elite world of private preparatory schools, coming from the right stock is essential; those born on the wrong side of the tracks often are excluded. David Greene (Brendan Fraser), a working-class teen on scholarship to an exclusive school, is widely accepted because of his football prowess, but he faces numerous struggles once the students find out his Jewish heritage.

David has taken a job serving in the school cafeteria. Recently his hallmates have learned that he is Jewish and they are saying disparaging things to him. Mimicking a sneeze, Richard (Anthony Rapp) says, "A Jew." He continues to make negative comments until David becomes physical with him. Chris (Chris O'Donnell) steps in and breaks it up. Richard says to him, "Look, my name is Richard Collins. What's yours, Reeseburg?" Later, David returns to the dormitory where he finds that someone has hung a sign with a swastika that reads "Go home, Jew." David rips it down and storms into the hallway where he hangs a poster challenging the person who hung the sign to meet him outside on the lawn. The scene ends with David outside standing in the rain.

> *School Ties* (Paramount Pictures, 1992), screenplay written by Dick Wolf & Darryl Ponicsanand directed by Robert Mandel
> Elapsed Time: This scene begins at 01:16:27 and ends at 01:19:07
> Rating: PG-13 for language

St. Vincent   HUMILIATION
Curmudgeonly neighbor, Vincent (Bill Murray) mentors his neighbor Oliver.

Oliver (Jaeden Lieberher) is being confronted in the locker room by several boys. Ocinski (Dario Barosso) calls Oliver a "little turd" just before a coach interrupts and sends them off to class. Oliver opens his locker to find his clothes have been stolen and he must conclude the day in his gym clothes.

> *St. Vincent* (Chernin Entertainment, 2014), written and directed by Theodore Melfi
> Elapsed Time: This scene begins at 16:48 and ends at 17:45
> Rating: Rated PG-13 for mature thematic material including sexual content, alcohol and tobacco use, and for language

St. Vincent   PHYSICAL/BYSTANDER
Curmudgeonly neighbor, Vincent (Bill Murray) mentors his neighbor Oliver.

Oliver (Jaeden Lieberher) is using the payphone when Ocinski (Dario Barrosso) and friends roll up on their skateboards. "Hey, look. It's dipshit. You live in this neighborhood?" Ocinski contends, "I probably got detention;cause of you, asshole." Oliver fires back, "You got detention 'cause you took my stuff." Ocinski pushes back, "How do you know I took it, you narc?" Oliver slaps Ocinski who pushes him down and steps on him. Ocinski charges, "Listen, the next time the teachers ask you what happened, you don't say anything, you got me? So, you can go crying to your mommy!" Vincent (Bill Murray) intervenes, "What are you little shit heels doing?" Vincent offers the boys, "I got a deal for you bully shit heels. Whatever you do to this guy here, I'm gonna do to your mothers. You understand? And in the meantime, ride this." Vincent breaks one of their skateboards across his knee and tells them to "Get moving, you little shits!"

> ***St. Vincent*** (Chernin Entertainment, 2014), written and directed by Theodore Melfi
> Elapsed Time: This scene begins at 31:00 and ends at 32:25
> Rating: Rated PG-13 for mature thematic material including sexual content, alcohol and tobacco use, and for language

Stand By Me   INTIMIDATION/PHYSICAL

Four boys hoping to find the body of a young teen who was recently killed by a train encounter a gang of bullies, guard dogs, and each other along the way.

Gordie (Wil Wheaton) and Chris (River Phoenix) encounter Ace (Kiefer Sutherland) and Eyeball (Bradley Gregg) outside a department store. Chris calls Ace a "real asshole" after Ace steals Gordie's hat. Ace offers "the opportunity of taking it back" threatening to burn Chris with a lit cigarette. Once Chris apologizes, Ace responds, "Now I feel a whole lot better about this. How about you?

> ***Stand By Me*** (Columbia Pictures Corporation), 1986, written by Raynold Gideon and directed by Rob Reiner
> Elapsed Time: This scene begins at 12:38 and ends at 13:45
> Rating: Rated R

Stand By Me   HUMILIATION/REVENGE

Four boys hoping to find the body of a young teen who was recently killed by a train encounter a gang of bullies, guard dogs, and each other along the way.

Gordie (Wil Wheaton) and friends are sharing stories around a campfire. Gordie shares a story about "a fat kid nobody likes named Davie Hogan. This kid is our age, but he's fat. Real fat. All the kids, instead of calling him Davie, they call him 'Lard Ass.' Lard Ass Hogan. Even his little brother and sister call him Lard Ass. At school, they put this sticker on his back that says 'wide load' and they rank him out and beat him up whenever they get a chance. But one day he gets an idea. The greatest revenge idea a kid ever had." The scene switches to Davie's revenge where they are announcing the contestants for the pie eating contest. When Davie is announced, Bill Travis (Dick Durock), the reigning champion, trips him. An audience member asks, "How was your trip, Lard Ass?" Bill warns Davie "Don't even think about winning this." Another audience member remarks, "Boy, are you fat." The pie eating contest commences and Davie seems to be a formidable contender. Gordie returns to his narration to tell that prior to the contest, Davie drank a bottle of castor oil—"What he wanted was revenge." Soon, Davie vomits which creates a chain reaction of vomiting across the crowd. "And Lard Ass just sat back and enjoyed what he'd created—a complete and total barfarama."

> ***Stand By Me*** (Columbia Pictures Corporation), 1986, written by Raynold Gideon and directed by Rob Reiner
> Elapsed Time: This scene begins at 42:32 and ends at 49:15
> Rating: Rated R

Standing Up   PHYSICAL/HUMILIATION
Howie (Chandler Canterbury) befriends Grace (Annalise Basso) after each is stripped naked during a camp prank. They run away and over the next three days learn a great deal about each other.

The scene begins as a female voice narrates. "Sometimes, popular kids can be really cruel. They can bully you into thinking that there's nothing special about you. They tried to do that to me at Camp Tall Pine. Thank God for sending me someone who changed my life." Soon, How (Chandler Canterbury) is sent to collect firewood. When he returns, none of the boys he had canoed with can be found. Moments later, Bryce (William T. Harrison) sneaks up behind him and puts him in a headlock. Bryce complains to the other boys, "Do I have to do everything by myself?" The boys strip all of Howie's clothes off and ask, "Don't you get it?" Walking away, a boy says to Bryce, "I don't think he gets it." Bryce answers, "Who cares?" A naked Howie wanders through the woods until he happens upon a cabin and begs Grace (Annalise Basso) to let him in. He begins to question, "They ditched you, too?" Grace had also been left with "a backpack with some junk in it." Howie admits, "So I guess we're this year's joke? They'll be back in the morning to laugh at us, I'm sure." Grace continues, "I hate them. I really hate them." Grace tells how she had been foiled. "We were going to desert Julia Christianson. We were supposed to go skinny dipping and we were going to ditch her. Howie ponders, "Ditch Julia Christianson? Isn't she kinda popular?" Grace cries, "I thought they liked me."

> ***Standing Up*** (AR Films, 2013), written and directed by D.J. Caruso
> Elapsed Time: This scene begins at 2:05 and ends at 9:33
> Rating: Rated PG for thematic elements including bullying, and for brief smoking and language

Step Brothers   **PHYSICAL**

When their parents marry each other, Dale (John C. Reilly) and Brennan (Will Ferrell), as adult children, must learn the meaning of blended families.

Dale (John C. Reilly) and Brennan (Will Ferrell) walking down the street and are confronted by Chris Gardocki (Logan Manus) and a group of other children. Chris states, "Let's make him lick dog shit." Chris calls Dale a "fag-stick" and wonders if Brennan is his "butt buddy." One child threatens, "If you don't come over here and lick that white dog shit, I'm gonna plow into your nose with my fist." Brennan responds, "I'm not licking any white dog shit, but Dale enters, "I'll lick the shit if you leave us alone." Brennan adds, "Dale, you're not licking dog shit okay? They're kids." The kids beat on the men and the scene ends when Brennan screams after licking the white turd.

> ***Step Brothers*** (Columbia Pictures, 2008), written and directed by Will Ferrell & Adam McKay
> Elapsed Time: This scene begins at 44:12 and ends at 45:19
> Rating: Rated R for crude and sexual content, and pervasive language

Superbad   **SOCIAL EXCLUSION/INTIMIDATION**

Super geeks Seth, Evan, and Fogell are on a quest for popularity and sexual conquest—each pledging to land their dream girls before they leave for college. To impress their prospective dates, they agree to get fake IDs and bring a buffet of liquor to a party. Can they reverse a lifetime of loserdom in just one night?

Seth (Jonah Hill) and Evan (Michael Cera) are looking at pornographic magazines in the local convenience store and discussing their lack of sexual experiences. They begin discussing potential hookups. Seth suggests that Evan's crush, Becca, looks to be a "good fucker...She looks like she can take a dick." Soon, the duo encounter Jesse (Scott Gerbacia) who is standing outside. Jesse questions Seth if he's heard about Jesse's grad party. Seth answers "no" just as Jesse spits a loogie onto Seth's shirt and tells him he's not invited. Additionally, neither is Seth's "fucking faggot friend" (referring to Evan). The scene ends as Seth and Evan debate who "bitched out."

> ***Superbad*** (Columbia Pictures, 2007), written by Seth Rogen & Evan Goldberg and directed by Greg Mottola
> Elapsed Time: This scene begins at 4:36 and ends at 7:41
> Rating: Rated R for pervasive crude and sexual content, strong language, drinking, some drug use and a fantasy/comic violent image—all involving teens

Ted   PHYSICAL/DISCRIMINATION

Since he was a child, John Bennett (Mark Wahlberg) has had difficulty making friends, except for his talking teddy bear, Ted (voiced by Seth McFarlane). Well, John is an adult and in a relationship with Lori Collins (Mila Kunis), and she expects him to stop playing with stuffed animals.

The film begins with the narrator announcing: "It's 1985 in a town just outside Boston. It was Christmas Eve and all the children were in high spirits. That special time of year when Boston children gather together and beat up the Jewish kids." A kid named Greenbaum is suddenly tackled by a bunch of neighborhood kids. Another kid named John Bennett asks to join in on the play and he is told to go away by all the kids—including Greenbaum.

> ***Ted*** (Universal Pictures, 2012), written and directed by Seth MacFarlane
> Elapsed Time: This scene begins at 00:01:02 and ends at 00:01:45
> Rating: Rated R for crude and sexual content, pervasive language, and some drug use

Temple Grandin   INTIMIDATION/BIAS

A dramatic biopic of Temple Grandin, an autistic woman who changed cattle herding techniques and earned a Ph.D. in animal husbandry.

Temple (Claire Danes) and her mother Eustacia (Julia Ormond) are visiting a residential school. While Eustacia talks with the admissions committee about

THE BIG SHORT   129

how Temple has been bullied and mistreated at other schools, Temple remains outside on the swings. Other children begin to make fun of Temple. Her mother sees this and prepares to rush outside but is stopped by Dr. Carlock (David Strathaim), the science teacher. The two chat about giving Temple a chance to learn and flourish. The scene ends as they admit that Temple is "Different, but not less."

> *Temple Grandin* (HBO FIlms, 2010), written by Christopher Monger & Merritt Johnson and directed by Mick Jackson
> Elapsed Time: This scene begins at 34:55 and ends at 39:29
> Rating: Rated TV-PG

Temple Grandin   INTIMIDATION/DISCRIMINATION
A dramatic biopic of Temple Grandin, an autistic woman who changed cattle herding techniques and earned a Ph.D. in animal husbandry.

Temple (Claire Danes) is working on building her go-kart. Soon Tim and another student barge in on her and rub something on her back while chanting "French fish, French fish" referencing an earlier occurrence in class. Temple punches Tim and is scolded by another teacher. She is punished and not allowed to ride for two weeks. The scene ends as Temple declares, "That's not fair."

> *Temple Grandin* (HBO FIlms, 2010), written by Christopher Monger & Merritt Johnson and directed by Mick Jackson
> Elapsed Time: This scene begins at 42:45 and ends at 43:50
> Rating: Rated TV-PG

Thirteen   PHYSICAL/INTIMIDATION
Life for Tracy (Evan Rachel Wood) gets so much more difficult as she turns thirteen and comes of age with her new friend, Evie (Nikki Reed). She discovers alcohol, drugs, and her own sexuality as he mother tries to cope with her rebellion and teen angst.

Tracy sits alone on the sidewalk when Yvette (Brandy Rainey) and another tough girl begin pushing her and calling her "Nasty" for getting "used" at a party. Tracy argues, "Shit never happened, but believe whatever the fuck you want." Tracy stands up to the girls who run away as the security team arrives. They declare "This shit ain't over!"

> ***Thirteen*** (Fox Searchlight Pictures, 2013), written by Catherine Hardwicke, Nikki Reed and directed by Catherine Hardwicke
> Elapsed Time: This scene begins at 1:24:30 and ends at 1:24:59
> Rating: Rated R for drug use, self destructive violence, language and sexuality—all involving young teens

Three O'Clock High   INTIMIDATION/PHYSICAL
Jerry Mitchell (Casey Siemaszko) runs afoul of the school bully, Buddy Revell (Richard Tyson) who promises to pummel Jerry at the end of the school day.

Jerry stands at the urinal when he realizes that Buddy is standing next to him. Jerry tries to make introductions, but Buddy interrupts, "If you're a fag..." Jerry explains that he works for the school newspaper and has been tasked to write a piece on Buddy being the new kid at school. Jerry mistakenly touches Buddy's shoulder—a definite No-No! Buddy physically assaults Jerry. Buddy argues that Jerry can "Take that newspaper of yours and wipe your dick off with it." Buddy threatens that he must work off his anger by fighting Jerry at 3:00. He warns, "You try and run, I'm gonna track you down. You go to a teacher, it's only gonna get worse. You sneak home, I'm gonna be under your bed." The scene ends as Buddy leaves the bathroom leaving Jerry a little shell-shocked.

> ***Three O'Clock High*** (Amblin Entertainment, 1987), written by Richard Christian Matheson & Tom Szolossiand, directed by Phil Joanou
> Elapsed Time: This scene begins at 14:09 and ends at 18:31
> Rating: Rated PG-13

Three O'Clock High   INTIMIDATION
Jerry Mitchell (Casey Siemaszko) runs afoul of the school bully, Buddy Revell (Richard Tyson) who promises to pummel Jerry at the end of the school day.

Jerry follows Buddy into the gymnasium and pleads with him to call off the fight. Jerry offers Buddy $350 to call off the fight. Buddy accepts saying, "You'll live." Buddy calls Jerry a "pussy" for not even trying to fight and questions "How does that feel?" as he exits the gym.

THE BIG SHORT   131

> *Three O'Clock High* (Amblin Entertainment, 1987), written by Richard Christian Matheson & Tom Szolossiand, directed by Phil Joanou
> Elapsed Time: This scene begins at 1:08:56 and ends at 1:11:09
> Rating: Rated PG-13

Three O'Clock High   INTIMIDATION/PHYSICAL

Jerry Mitchell (Casey Siemaszko) runs afoul of the school bully, Buddy Revell (Richard Tyson) who promises to pummel Jerry at the end of the school day.

The school bell rings at 3:00 and Jerry appears outside to the cheers and adulation of his fellow students. Mr. O'Rourke (John P. Ryan) announces there will be no fight. The students boo. They came to see a fight! Buddy knocks O'Rourke unconscious with one punch. Jerry gets in a few good punches but is overpowered by Buddy who brandishes brass knuckles. A female student tells Jerry to "cripple the dick!" Even Mr. O'Rourke argues "Don't fuck this up, Mitchell!" Jerry manages to get the brass knuckles and knocks Buddy unconscious.

> *Three O'Clock High* (Amblin Entertainment, 1987), written by Richard Christian Matheson & Tom Szolossiand, directed by Phil Joanou
> Elapsed Time: This scene begins at 1:13:42 and ends at 1:21:26
> Rating: Rated PG-13

Tormented   PHYSICAL/INTIMIDATION

A bullying victim commits suicide but comes back from the dead to torments his bullies.

Jason (Olly Alexander) is running away from Bradley (Alex Pettyfer) and Marcus (Tom Hopper). They corner him in the gymnasium dragging him on the floor. Marcus lifts him up and slams him against the wall. Calling him a "plucky little fucker," Bradley accuses Jason of sending text messages from Mullet's, the dead student, phone. Marcus gives Jason an atomic wedgie lifting Jason off the floor by his underwear. Bradley adds "Jason, you're only hurting yourself, mate" and punches Jason in the face. The boys receive a text again from Mullet. It's clear that Jason is not the culprit, but Bradley cites, "I don't give a fuck. He gets on my tits anyway." Soon, the gym teacher interrupts and sends Brad and Marcus away. He chides Jason saying "Kids like you make me sick" and gives Jason detention for the rest of the week.

Tormented (BBC Films, 2009), written by Stephen Prentice, directed by Jon Wright
Elapsed Time: This scene begins at 29:56 and ends at 33:09
Rating: Rated R

Tormented REVENGE

A bullying victim commits suicide but comes back from the dead to torments his bullies.

Marcus (Tom Hopper) is taking a shower in the school's locker room. He receives a text message saying "You're a dumb fuck." Speaking aloud, Marcus states, "If someone's dicking me about..." Standing naked in the mirror, he wipes the steam off the mirror and the dead Mullet stands there watching him. Mullet snaps him repeatedly with a towel and Marcus hits him with a cricket bat. Mullet regains consciousness and Marcus runs away having barely put his underwear on. When he reaches the fence, he presumes he is safe, but Mullet grabs him by the underwear and impales him on the fence.

Tormented (BBC Films, 2009), written by Stephen Prentice, directed by Jon Wright
Elapsed Time: This scene begins at 58:14 and ends at 1:02:25
Rating: Rated R

Tormented INTIMIDATION

A bullying victim commits suicide but comes back from the dead to torments his bullies.

Nasser (James Floyd) walks down the hallway talking about music with a couple friends. Bradley (Alex Petterfer) grabs Nasser and pins him against the wall. He warns Nasser to take down a webpage he created. Nasser tries to tell Brad about his music creation, but Brad adds "I don't give a shit about your emo tit-wank. I want the site down, and I want it done today, because if it ain't, well, you won't need to self-harm, cause I'll be doing it for you. Clear?" Nasser claims, "Yeah, I was—I was planning to do it anyway. A piece of piss, Brad."

Tormented (BBC Films, 2009), written by Stephen Prentice, directed by Jon Wright
Elapsed Time: This scene begins at 21:00 and ends at 21:52
Rating: Rated R

THE BIG SHORT   133

Tormented   VERBAL/INTIMIDATION

A bullying victim commits suicide but comes back from the dead to torments his bullies.

Several students are in a room and talking about the recent murders. One female student says, "Mullet said he was going to kill them, and now he has." Alex (Dmitri Leonidas) affirms, "Well, we did treat him like shit." Brad (Alex Pettyfer) shouts, "It's not Darren Mullet! For fuck's sake. Am I the only one who can see this?" Justine (Tuppence Middleton) wonders why people picked on Mullet. Sophie (Georgia King) defends, "You want to know why we picked on him? We were bored. He was a spaz. You do the math." Justine argues, "I'm glad I'm not like you." Sophie counters, Oh, suck my cock, you prissy bitch. You look down your nose at everyone, but you spread your legs just like the rest of us." Justine and Sophie begin fighting and Justine is thrown into the pool. The scene ends as Sophie declares, "This isn't over! You're dead!"

> *Tormented* (BBC Films, 2009), written by Stephen Prentice, directed by Jon Wright
> Elapsed Time: This scene begins at 1:02:33 and ends at 1:04:02
> Rating: Rated R

Tormented   INTIMIDATION

A bullying victim commits suicide but comes back from the dead to torments his bullies.

The scene opens upon the drawing of an ejaculating penis on the chalkboard reading "Bradley White is a knob gobbler." Bradley (Alex Pettyfer) goes around the classroom wondering who drew the image. He asks, "What fucker wrote this?" He accosts a male student and mandates that he go clean off the board. Just then, Brad receives text message with a smiling emoji simulating oral sex on a pencil. He closes his phone stating emphatically, "Jason Banks is a dead man."

> *Tormented* (BBC Films, 2009), written by Stephen Prentice, directed by Jon Wright
> Elapsed Time: This scene begins at 22:33 and ends at 23:11
> Rating: Rated R

Tormented   INTIMIDATION

A bullying victim commits suicide but comes back from the dead to torments his bullies.

Alex (Dmitri Leonidas) and Justine (Tuppence Middleton) are viewing a video posted to a website showing how Darren Mullet was bullied. The video begins as if it were a nature documentary. "Now, here we see the lesser spotted Mullet and feeding time." Students are throwing items at Mullet (Calvin Dean) as he tries to eat. Later, Darren is in the shower receiving jabs and pokes from other male students. The video picks up on "the courtship rituals of the Mullet." The narrator states, "Ooh, the Mullet's fallen for a very rare species [referring to Darren's crush on Justine]. Head girlus frigidus bitchus. Now let's see what happens. " Bradley (Alex Pettyfer) and others push Darren into Justine who is on the telephone. Darren begins having an asthma attack but the other students play keep away with his inhaler. Darren cries out for Justine's help, but she is oblivious. As he struggles to breathe, Marcus (Tom Hopper) spins him around and makes him smile for the camera. Marcus continues taunting, "Breathe, piggy. Breathe, piggy." Alex tries to defend himself to an irate Justine, "Juss, I'm not like them, okay?" Justine counters "No, you're some much worse. At least Bradley's honest about who he is." Alex continues, "You don't understand. Okay, nobody ever says no to Bradley. I didn't have a choice. Justine ejects Alex from her house.

> ***Tormented*** (BBC Films, 2009), written by Stephen Prentice, directed by Jon Wright
> Elapsed Time: This scene begins at 1:05:02 and ends at 1:08:02)
> Rating: Rated R

Tormented   INTIMIDATION

A bullying victim commits suicide but comes back from the dead to torments his bullies.

Justine (Tuppence Middleton) is being accosted by several other girls. A text message of an emoji being covered in poop declares, "Help! I'm lost in your ass." Khalillah (Larissa Wilson) declares "It's that she-male Helena." Another girl adds, "Yeah, I heard she said you were any ugly bitch at the funeral. And that you had chubby thighs. Natasha (April Pearson) argues her frustration saying, "Yeah, it's beginning to get right up my ass." The girls corner Helena

(Mary Nighy) in the bathroom where they say she smells like poo and they wonder if she is having a "wank" [masturbating]. When she emerges from the stall, the girls restrain Helena and continue their assault. Natasha calls Helena a "stupid, geeky, little bitch" and a "twisted, dyke slut." Natasha destroys Helena's cell phone before they exit the bathroom.

> *Tormented* (BBC Films, 2009), written by Stephen Prentice, directed by Jon Wright
> Elapsed Time: This scene begins at 41:36 and ends at 44:25
> Rating: Rated R

Tormented   INTIMIDATION
A bullying victim commits suicide but comes back from the dead to torments his bullies.

Jason (Olly Alexander) and Justine (Tuppence Middleton) are discussing what the climate at school was like for Darren Mullet. Jason wonders, "I bet you like coming to school. Don't you? You've got no idea what it's like to be bullied, do you?" He explains, "Darren couldn't escape, even when he was at home. They sent him texts and emails, and they set up a website. And what's he supposed to do? You tell a teacher, and they tell the bullies off, and that gives them an excuse to come after you. You tell your parents, and they say, 'Stand up for yourself.' Darren couldn't stand up for himself."

> *Tormented* (BBC Films, 2009), written by Stephen Prentice, directed by Jon Wright
> Elapsed Time: This scene begins at 37:54 and ends at 41:25
> Rating: Rated R

Tracey Fragments, The   PHYSICAL/HUMILIATION
Tracey's life is a little weird. Even though she's naked, she must search for her younger brother—who thinks he's a dog.

Tracey (Ellen Page) narrates as she is pushed and tripped several times in the school hallway. An unnamed boy starts, "Well, look who it is. It's the titless wonder." Tracey begins, "This is the story of the girl with no tits. Went to my school. No tits. Big dumb moon face." She is passed a note calling her several perjoratives. Her teacher yells at her to throw the note away.

> *The Tracey Fragments* (Shadow Shows, 2007), written by Maureen Medved, directed by Bruce McDonald
> Elapsed Time: This scene begins at 11:23 and ends at 13:00
> Rating: Rated R for strong language throughout, some sexual content and violence

Unfriended   CYBERBULLYING/HUMILIATION

Laura commits suicide after experiencing bullying. Has she found a way to communicate online with her former friends?

Blaire (Shelley Hennig) is being confronted online by the ghost impersonating her dead friend, Laura. Blaire wonders why the spirit is tormenting her, but the spirit displays an online video on Facebook of Blaire making fun of a drunk and passed out Laura. Laura has defecated on herself and Blaire points and laughs "I got her."

> *Unfriended* (Bazelevs Production, 2014), written by Nelson Greaves, directed by Levan Gabriadze
> Elapsed Time: This scene begins at 1:14:02 and ends at 1:16:11
> Rating: Rated R for violent content, pervasive language, some sexuality, and drug and alcohol use—all involving teens

Unfriended   CYBERBULLYING

Laura commits suicide after experiencing bullying. Has she found a way to communicate online with her former friends?

A group of friends are in a video chat room. They invite Val (Courtney Halverson) into the chat. Soon, pictures appear on Val's Facebook page of Val at a party drinking and using drugs. The pictures appear to be posted from Jess's account. Jess (Renee Olmstead) argues that she did not post them. Val explodes calling Jess a "trashy little bitch" and a litany of other pejoratives. The two girls continue to argue and curse each other out until another person using Laura's account chimes in. Laura is dead.

> *Unfriended* (Bazelevs Production, 2014), written by Nelson Greaves, directed by Levan Gabriadze
> Elapsed Time: This scene begins at 18:53 and ends at 24:51
> Rating: Rated R for violent content, pervasive language, some sexuality, and drug and alcohol use—all involving teens

THE BIG SHORT   137

Varsity Blues   INTIMIDATION
In a small town in Texas, there is one phenomenon binding the entire town—high school football. The only route to success is on the gridiron, and fate brings popularity for one second string quarterback, Jonathan "Mox" Moxon (James Van Der Beek), when the star quarterback is injured.

Billy Bob (Ron Lester) is a gentle giant; he has a larger than life personality and physical frame to match. He is the main defensive lineman for the football team and has taken his share of tough hits on the field. While in class, Billy Bob faints and is taken to the school nurse. Coach Kilmer (Jon Voight) tells him to ignore the nurse's advice to skip the next game because "She doesn't have no division title to win." In fact, the coach tells Billy he will "play every minute of that game." Coach Kilmer continues, "I'm gonna ask you, son, are you ready to go?" Billy Bob affirms. "That's my soldier, William Robert." He tells Billy to rest and show up at practice.

> *Varsity Blues* (Paramount Pictures, 1999), written by W. Peter Iliff, directed by Brian Robbins
> Elapsed Time: This scene begins at 27:00 and ends at 28:15
> Rating: Rated R for strong language throughout, sexuality and nudity, and some substance abuse

A Walk to Remember   HAZING
Jamie Sullivan (Mandy Moore) has learned that she has terminal cancer and makes a list of things she wishes to do before she dies. She is a devout Christian who values helping others less fortunate. Landon Carter (Shane West), a popular boy in her high school, regularly makes fun of her—until he needs her help. The two fall in love, are married, and pledge a love that will last a lifetime.

Landon Carter (Shane West) has arrived at a secluded quarry where he and his friends hang out drinking and smooching. He and his friends have plans to prank a new kid into jumping from a water tower. When a female teen scolds them for their plans, Dean (Clayne Crawford) retorts, "You've talked shit the whole time here. Why don't you be quiet?" Landon intervenes, "You know how it is. Nobody's forcing him to show up." Their target arrives and Dean explains, "Okay, here's the deal. You're gonna jump from up there into here [a reservoir below]. That's it, and you're one of us. Okay?" When the young boy gets hurt on the jump, the teens abandon him on the bank.

> *A Walk to Remember* (Warner Brothers, 2002), written by Karen Janszen, directed by Adam Shankman
> Elapsed Time: This scene begins at 0:58 and ends at 7:25
> Rating: Rated PG for thematic elements, language and some sensual material

Weird Science   HUMILIATION

Unpopular with the ladies, two nerds invent a woman on their computers to be a sex slave.

Wyatt (Ilan Mitchell-Smith) and Gary (Anthony Michael Hall) are standing at the threshold of the gymnasium admiring the young ladies in the class. Wyatt admits, "Nobody likes us. Nobody." When they make comments about the girlfriends of Ian (Robert Downey, Jr.) and Max (Robert Rusler), the two boys are irritated. Ian and Max sneak up behind Gary and Wyatt and pants them; the duo yell, "Yo, check us out!" The population in the gym turn to the boys now in their underpants. The boys exit in shame.

> *Weird Science* (Universal Pictures, 1985), written and directed by John Hughes
> Elapsed Time: This scene begins at 0:18 and ends at 2:25
> Rating: Rated PG for thematic elements, language and some sensual material

Weird Science   HUMILIATION

Unpopular with the ladies, two nerds invent a woman on their computers to be a sex slave.

Wyatt (Ilan Mitchell-Smith) and Gary (Anthony Michael Hall) are seated near the fountain in the mall chatting about how life has gotten better now that they have Lisa. On the level above them, Ian and Max prepare to pour a red slushie on their heads—against the wishes of their girlfriends who plead for them to be more mature. Unbeknownst, Wyatt states, "You know, Gar, for the first time in my life. I don't feel like a total dick." Just then, it rains red Icee and the surrounding crowd erupts with laughter. Deb (Suzanne Snyder) complains, "I'm getting really bored of their shit." The scene ends as the girls agree to forgive Ian amd Max.

> *Weird Science* (Universal Pictures, 1985), written and directed by John Hughes
> Elapsed Time: This scene begins at 32:29 and ends at 34:06
> Rating: Rated PG for thematic elements, language and some sensual material

Welcome to the Dollhouse — SOCIAL EXCLUSION/BYSTANDER

Rejected by her friends and family, Dawn is threatened by a school delinquent who promises to rape her at 3:00.

Dawn (Heather Matarazzo) is standing in the cafeteria trying to locate a place to sit. When she eyes an open seat, she heads towards it, but another student claims the seat. She finds a seat near a loner student and sits down. Soon, several cheerleaders confront her and ask if she's a lesbian. When she denies, the girls walk away chanting "Lesbo, Lesbo, Lesbo." Later, while standing at her locker, she overhears a younger male student being assaulted by older male students. They declare, "Fag! You're a faggot! Aren't you? Admit it. I'm a faggot. Say it!" One of the boys, after knocking the books from his hand, tells the victim, "You look beautiful in this suit, Troy. You fuckin' faggot. You're a faggot, aren't you, Troy-boy?" Dawn tries to intervene, but the boys ignore her and call her "Wienerdog" and "dogface." Brandon (Brendan Sexton) questions, "What's the matter, ugly? You like faggots?" The boys leave the hallway and Dawn steps in to comfort Troy who declares, "Leave me alone, Wienerdog" and runs away.

> ***Welcome to the Dollhouse*** (Suburban Pictures, 1995), written and directed by Todd Solondz
> Elapsed Time: This scene begins at 1:51 and ends at 5:08
> Rating: Rated R for language

You Again — HUMILIATION

Marni (Kristen Bell) was a stereotypical nerd and outcast in high school. She meets her brother's fiancée only to learn she is her high school bully. Now 30 years old and more sure of herself, Marni plots revenge.

Marni (Kristen Bell) is on an airplane telephone talking to her mother, Gail (Jamie Lee Curtis) about her brother's upcoming wedding. Gail informs Marni that her soon-to-be sister-in-law, JJ, is the same girl who bullied Marni in high school. The scene cuts to a montage of memories of maltreatment. Marni is detained by an air marshall (played by Dwayne "The Rock" Johnson). When Marni finishes telling the marshall her story, he shares this wisdom, "Marni, let me tell you about bullies. They're just like terrorists, only they're emotional terrorists. You can never let them get the upper hand, so the best thing you can do in this situation is remain calm and show her that you are in control."

> ***You Again*** (Touchstone Pictures, 2010), written by Moe Jelline and directed by Andy Fickman
> Elapsed Time: This scene begins at 6:30 and ends at 9:35
> Rating: Rated PG for brief mild language and rude behavior

You Again   **HUMILIATION/REVENGE**

Marni (Kristen Bell) was a stereotypical nerd and outcast in high school. She meets her brother's fiancée only to learn she is her high school bully. Now 30 years old and more sure of herself, Marni plots revenge.

To exact her revenge on JJ (Odette Annable), Marni (Kristen Bell) unearths a video from a high school time capsule showing JJ proudly confessing to be the "warden" of their high school "prison." In the video, JJ declares, "In high school, only the strong survive. The meek shall not inherit the earth." After mooing Marni away, JJ states, "High school's a four year sentence. They don't let you out early for good behavior. So, take it from me, it's better to be bad."

> ***You Again*** (Touchstone Pictures, 2010), written by Moe Jelline and directed by Andy Fickman
> Elapsed Time: This scene begins at 1:11:12 and ends at 1:12:42
> Rating: Rated PG for brief mild language and rude behavior

You Again   **HUMILIATION/SOCIAL EXCLUSION**

Marni (Kristen Bell) was a stereotypical nerd and outcast in high school. She meets her brother's fiancée only to learn she is her high school bully. Now 30 years old and more sure of herself, Marni plots revenge.

Marni (Kristen Bell) is recording a video for her senior year time capsule. She recounts how life is hard for her. The scene cuts to a memory where she is locked out of the school by JJ (Odette Annable) and friends as they sing "We are the Champions" by Queen. Dejected, Marni sits on the stoop at the school.

> ***You Again*** (Touchstone Pictures, 2010), written by Moe Jelline and directed by Andy Fickman
> Elapsed Time: This scene begins at 00:22 and ends at 1:40
> Rating: Rated PG for brief mild language and rude behavior

Zootopia   **INTIMIDATION/PHYSICAL**

Hopps the bunny wants nothing more than to be a police officer. She learns of a conspiracy to frame carnivorous animals.

Gideon Grey (voiced by Phil Johnston) is harassing smaller animals for prize tickets on the playground. Judy Hopps (voiced by Ginnifer Godwin), dressed in a police uniform, attempts to intervene. Gideon forcefully pushes Hopps and challenges, "You scared now? Look at her nose twitch. She is scared. Cry little baby bunny." Just then, Hopps kicks Gideon who lashes back and scratches Hopps' face. Gideon pins Hopps down and states, "I want you to remember this moment the next time you think you will ever be more than just a stupid, carrot-farming, dumb bunny" and walks away. The other animals rush to Judy's aid.

> *Zootopia* (Walt Disney Pictures, 2016), written by Moe Jared Bush & Phil Johnston and directed by Byron Howard, Rich Moore, & Jared Bush
> Elapsed Time: This scene begins at 4:15 and ends at 5:48
> Rating: Rated PG

CHAPTER 11

This Is the End
Conclusion

Perhaps as an off-shoot of Mean World Syndrome, it is interesting to note how many films centered on the theme of bullying released after the Columbine shooting (April, 1999) include a plot line where the targeted victim sets a revenge plan in motion that includes murdering the people who have bullied them. What are our children learning from the films they consume? However violent the culture, it is not wise for educators to hide their heads in the sand hoping things would change. They must actively help students develop the citizenship skills that create the atmosphere to empower students to look out for one another.

In the film The Switch (2010), Wally (Jason Bateman) secretly substitutes his own sperm for his best friend and secret crush Kassie (Jennifer Aniston), who is trying to get pregnant. When the child is born with striking similarities and quirks, Wally must decide to tell the truth about the conception. As he is getting to know Kassie's son, Sebastian, Wally and Sebastian (Thomas Robinson) are talking and Wally inquires about Sebastian's experiences in school. Sebastian's lack of response prompts Wally to ask "What's his name?" Wally admits "I've been there." Wally pushes, "You know you're going to have to stand up to him sooner or later, right?" Sebastian says "I don't want to." Wally counters, "Well then, he's probably going to kick your ass." Wally tells him to "act crazy" so that no one messes with him.

The advice to "act crazy" mimics the revenge attitude. We don't want/need students to be looking for ways and reasons to harm one another, but to encourage and affirm one another. Perhaps one solution to the national bullying crisis comes from the film *Drillbit Taylor* (2008). Wade (Nate Hartley), Ryan (Troy Gentile), and Emmitt (David Dorfman) have been skipping school to avoid their bullies. They are meeting with Drillbit (Owen Wilson) who shares the secret to curb the bully. "If you're not ready to fight, there is another alternative. But, I've got to be honest with you, only the strongest of warriors can pull this one off…most men tremble at its mere thought…love him." Ryan counters, "I don't know what's going through your head Drillbit, but I'm not gonna bang him." Drillbit argues, "When I'm talking about love, I mean compassion and understanding. Find your commonality. Let him know you're more alike than different. Maybe that'll put out his fuse."

Many have said (believed) that there will never be an end to bullying. We disagree. We believe that by empowering kids to speak up for themselves and their peers—as victims or bystanders—we can create a culture of affirmation rather than destruction. Teachers, as the front line managers and pivotal "first responders" can give empower students and give them the lexicon and thereby the voice to talk confidently about the school's climate. We hope that the youth will come to trust you, Teacher, to come to the defense and aid of the targeted victims of bullies and tell you or some other authority figure about what they've witnessed. We try to keep in mind that someone's life or livelihood hangs in the balance.

Film Index

2:37   24, 52
17 Again   64

About a Boy   64
Accepted   64, 65
Agent Cody Banks   65
American Bully   56, 65–67
American Teen   13, 67
Andre   68
Anger Management   52, 68, 69

Back to the Future   21
Back to the Future, Part II   21
Back to the Future, Part III   21
Back to the Future, Part III   21
Bang Bang, You're Dead   53
Benchwarmers, The   25, 62, 69
Boy Next Door, The   70
Boys Don't Cry   14
Bridge to Terabithia, The   52, 70, 71
Brotherhood, The   71, 72
Buried Alive   72

Can't Hardly Wait   72–73
Carrie   28, 73, 74
Central Intelligence   34, 74
Charlie Bartlett   74, 75
Christmas Story, A   22, 52, 75, 76
Chronicle   76
Cider House Rules   36
Clique, The   76
College   77, 78
Contest   ix, 47, 78
Craft, The   78, 79
Cursed   14, 79, 80
Cyberbully   15, 81
D3: The Mighty Ducks   81, 82
Dazed & Confused   83
Diary of a Wimpy Kid   84
Dodgeball: A True Underdog
    Story   24, 84
Drillbit Taylor   35, 84–86
Drumline   86

Ella Enchanted   87

Fat Boy Chronicles   34, 88
Final, The   30, 33, 88–93
First Kid   93
Flirting   93, 94
Freedom Writers   57

Geography Club   14, 94
Girl Like Her, A   16, 41, 96
Going Greek   96, 97

Hangman's Curse   97
Hearts in Atlantis   97, 98
Holes   98
Hot Chick, The   99
How to Eat Fried Worms   99, 100

Invisible, The   100, 101

JFK   37–38
Joe Somebody   101
Just One of the Guys   23, 102, 103

Karate Kid II, The   104
Karate Kid, The   23, 103
Killer Klowns from Outer Space   104

Let Me In   24, 105–106
Little Rascals, The   19, 106
Lord of the Flies, The   57, 106, 107
Love Don't Cost a Thing   27, 107
Lucas   107–108

Martian Child   109
Matilda   109, 110
Max Keeble's Big Move   20, 110, 111
Mean Creek   111, 112
Mean Girls   27, 112, 113
Meatballs   113
My Bodyguard   21, 113, 114

Napoleon Dynamite   114, 115
Not Another Teen Movie   27, 115

Odd Girl Out   27, 33, 115, 116
Odd Life of Timothy Green, The   117

Perks of Being a Wallflower, The   30, 118
Pitch Perfect   1
Powder   118, 119
Prom   120

Radio   25, 120
Read It and Weep   26, 120, 121
Return to Sleepaway Camp   121
Rocky V   122, 123

School Ties   123, 124
Slumdog Millionaire   33, 88
St. Vincent   124, 125
Stand by Me   22, 125, 126
Standing Up   126, 127
Stepbrothers   25, 127
Superbad   128
Switch, The   142

Ted   128

Temple Grandin   129
Thirteen   129
Three O'Clock High   13, 20, 130, 131
Tormented   131–135
Toy Story   20
Tracey Fragments, The   135, 136

Unfriended   13, 136

Varsity Blues   137

Wag the Dog   37
Walk to Remember, A   137, 138
Weird Science   138
Welcome to the Dollhouse   23, 139

You Again   26, 140

Zootopia   141

Films by Definition

Aggression
Cursed   79, 80
Let Me In   105, 106
Mean Creek   111

Bias
2:37   62
American Bully   65
Cursed   79, 80
Flirting   93, 94
Geography Club   94
Temple Grandin   128

Bystander
Benchwarmers, The   61, 69
Boy Next Door, The   70
Central Intelligence   74
Drillbit Taylor   84, 85
Final, The   92
Karate Kid, The   103
Karate Kid II, The   104
Lucas 107
Max Keeble's Big Move   110
Perks of Being a
    Wallflower, The   117
St. Vincent   124
Welcome to the Dollhouse   139

Cyberbullying
American Teen   67
Cyberbully   81
Girl Like Her, A   94, 95
Odd Girl Out   116
Unfriended   136

Discrimination
American Bully   66
Craft, The   78, 79
Final, The   88
Radio 120
School Ties   123, 124
Ted 128
Temple Grandin   129
Thirteen   129, 130

Harassment
2:37   62
About a Boy   64
American Bully   65, 66
Cursed   79, 80
D3: The Mighty Ducks   81, 82
Dazed & Confused   83
Ella Enchanted   87

Hazing
Accepted   64, 65
Brotherhood, The   71, 72
Buried Alive   72
College   77
Dazed & Confused   83
Drumline   86
Going Greek   96, 97
Perks of Being a
    Wallflower, The   118
Powder   118
Prom 120
Walk to Remember, A   137

Humiliation
Accepted   64, 65
Anger Management   68
Brotherhood, The   71, 72
Buried Alive   72
Carrie 73
Central Intelligence   74
Final, The   88
Geography Club   94
Going Greek   96
Hot Chick, The   99
How to Eat Fried Worms   100
Lucas 108
Matilda   109
Max Keeble's Big Move   110
Prom 120
Radio 120
Return to Sleepaway Camp   121
St. Vincent   124
Stand by Me   125, 126
Standing Up   126, 127

Tracey Fragments, The	135
Unfriended	136
Weird Science	138
You Again	139, 140

Intimidation

Bridge to Terabithia, The	70, 71
Christmas Story, A	75
Cursed	79, 80
D3: The Mighty Ducks	81, 82
Diary of a Wimpy Kid	83
Dodgeball: A True Underdog Story	84
Drillbit Taylor	86
Fat Boy Chronicles, The	87
Girl Like Her, A	95
Hangman's Curse	97
Hearts in Atlantis	97, 98
Joe Somebody	101
Just One of the Guys	101, 102
Karate Kid II, The	104
Killer Klowns from Outer Space	104
Let Me In	106
Little Rascals, The	106
Lord of the Flies, The	106, 107
Lucas 107	
Martian Child	108, 109
Matilda	109
Max Keeble's Big Move	111
Mean Creek	112
Meatballs	113
My Bodyguard	113–115
Powder	118, 119
Return to Sleepaway Camp	121
Stand by Me	125
Superbad	127, 128
Temple Grandin	128, 129
Thirteen	131
Three O'Clock High	130, 131
Tormented	131–135
Varsity Blues	137
Zootopia	141

Physical

17 Again	63
American Bully	65, 66
Anger Management	68
Benchwarmers, The	61, 69
Carrie 73	

Charlie Bartlett	74, 75
Christmas Story, A	75
Chronicle	76
College	77
Contest	78
Cursed	79, 80
D3: The Mighty Ducks	82
Dazed & Confused	83
Diary of a Wimpy Kid	83
Dodgeball: A True Underdog Story	84
Drillbit Taylor	84–86
Final, The	88
First Kid	93
Geography Club	94
Girl Like Her, A	94, 95
Hangman's Curse	97
Hearts in Atlantis	97, 98
Holes 98	
How to Eat Fried Worms	99, 100
Invisible, The	100, 101
Joe Somebody	101
Just One of the Guys	101, 102
Karate Kid, The	103
Let Me In	105, 106
Lord of the Flies, The	106, 107
Love Don't Cost a Thing	107
Lucas 108	
Martian Child	108, 109
Max Keeble's Big Move	110
Mean Creek	111, 112
My Bodyguard	114
Napoleon Dynamite	114
Odd Life of Timothy Green, The	117
Perks of Being a Wallflower, The	117
Powder	119
Return to Sleepaway Camp	121
Rocky V	122
St. Vincent	124
Stand by Me	125
Standing Up	126, 127
Stepbrothers	127
Ted 128	
Thirteen	129, 130
Three O'Clock High	130, 131
Tormented	131
Tracey Fragments, The	135
Zootopia	141

FILMS BY DEFINITION

Revenge

17 Again	63
Agent Cody Banks	65
Anger Management	68, 69
Can't Hardly Wait	72, 73
Carrie	73
D3: The Mighty Ducks	82
Final, The	88–92
Killer Klowns from Outer Space	104
Let Me In	105
Rocky V	122, 123
Stand by Me	125, 126
Tormented	132
You Again	140

Social Exclusion

Andre	68
Clique, The	76
Craft, The	78, 79
Flirting	93, 94
Love Don't Cost a Thing	107
Mean Girls	112
Not Another Teen Movie	115
Odd Girl Out	115, 116
Read It & Weep	120
Superbad	127, 128
Welcome to the Dollhouse	139
You Again	140

Verbal

Boy Next Door, The	70
Bridge to Terabithia, The	70, 71
Craft, The	78, 79
Cursed	80
Ella Enchanted	87
Fat Boy Chronicles, The	87
Not Another Teen Movie	115
School Ties	123, 124
Tormented	133
You Again	142

Term Index

Anti-Bullying   x, 9, 29, 45–51, 53, 57, 58

Belief Change   8
Bloom's Taxonomy   1, 2, 9, 10, 12
   affective domain   2, 4, 5
   cognitive domain   1–3, 5
Bully-Free Zones   31
Bullying
   types of
   cyber   15–17, 43, 47–50, 67, 81, 116, 136
   physical   vii, 5, 13, 14, 16, 17, 28, 29, 33, 39, 63, 66, 68, 69, 73–79, 83–87, 93–95, 97–103, 105–108, 110–114, 117, 119, 121–131, 135, 141,
   social   vii, ix, 13, 19, 25–27, 41, 54–56, 61, 68, 69, 73, 74, 78, 93, 107, 115, 116, 120, 127, 139
   verbal   vii, 13, 14, 17, 70, 78, 87, 115, 123, 133
ByStander   x, 24, 29, 30, 31, 56, 61, 69, 70, 74, 85, 93, 104, 107, 110, 124, 139, 143
Bystander Effect   vii, 29

Cyberbullying Research Center   15, 49

Dan Olweus   24
Dear Colleague Letter   32
Deliberate Indifference   44

Gelotophia   40, 42

Harassment   vii, 16, 18, 36, 41, 43, 44, 48, 57, 62, 64–66, 80, 81, 83, 87, 95, 118, 119

Instructional Activities   9

Lesbian, Gay, Bisexual and Transgendered (LGBT)   13, 45

National Center for Education Statistics   13, 14, 15

Psychomotor Skills   5

Social Capital   27, 107
Social Exclusion   vii, 27, 68, 76, 78, 94, 107, 113, 115, 116, 120, 127, 139
Substantial Disruption   44, 45

Targets   13–15, 22, 26, 30, 32, 33
The Bully Police   45
Tinker Test   44

Vulnerable Populations   13

U.S. Department of Education   vii, 15, 32, 47

Printed in the United States
By Bookmasters